Berkshire Trails

for Walking and Ski Touring

by Whit Griswold

drawings by Jane Ashley
cover by Eric Von Schmidt

Copyright 1979 by Fast & McMillan Publishers, Inc.

First Printing

Library of Congress Cataloging in Publication Data

Griswold, Whit, 1944-
    Berkshire trails for walking and ski touring.

    Bibliography: p.
1. Hiking—Massachusetts—Berkshire Hills—Guide-books. 2. Cross-country skiing—Massachusetts—Berkshire Hills—Guide-books. 3. Berkshire Hills, Mass.—Description and travel—Guide-books.
I. Title.
GV199.42.M42B473   917.44'1   79-4901
ISBN 0-914788-13-2

Cover design by Eric Von Schmidt.
Drawings by Jane Ashley.
Maps by Sarah Leahy and Whit Griswold.

Typography by Raven Type.
Printed in the United States of America by The Delmar Company.

The East Woods Press
820 East Boulevard
Charlotte, NC 28203

About the Author

Whit Griswold attended a boarding school in the Berkshires where, he confesses, he spent more time outdoors than in the classroom. He then cooped himself up long enough to earn degrees from Yale and John Hopkins. He is co-author with J.H. Mitchell of *Hiking Cape Cod*. In addition to freelance writing, he has worked as teacher, political organizer and fishing guide.

Acknowledgments

Many, many thanks to Jane Ashley for her fine illustrations; to Eric Von Schmidt for his lively cover; to Dan Hart and Charles Quinlan for their research and writing in the chapter, Natural History; to Sally McMillan and Molly Killingsworth, the editors who pushed me to the top of the hill and polished my technique on the way down; to Sarah Leahy for her meticulous work on the maps; to Cheri Sheaff for typing most of the final draft; to Sherry Gaherty and her colleagues at the Lenox Public Library; to Lawrence Wickander and the staff of the Williams College Library; to many helpful employees of the Massachusetts Department of Environmental Management, especially Carl Curtin and Dave Carlon; to Greg and Jennifer Goggins, Edward and Elizabeth Childs, and Sandy and Susan Lord, all of whom put me up when I was stranded; and finally to Laura Wainwright, who put up with me when the chips were down, and to whom this book is dedicated.

Contents

An Old Friend

Before the warmth of the sun had chased away the last of the lingering ground fog from the previous night, I found myself driving south along Route 8 in Cheshire one morning last July. I pulled the car onto the road shoulder to have a look at a stand of trees that I could not identify. As I reached into the back seat for my binoculars, I spotted a man who was already at work pruning some bushes about fifty yards up the road. I hoped that he would not notice me as I crossed a small clearing to get a better look at the trees. I felt like a fool standing at the base of one of the trees—looking straight up her skirts, you might say—and waiting for the light breeze to ease up for a moment so that I could get a good look at a leaf. But before I had focused the glasses, I heard him behind me. I anticipated a clever remark like, "Most of the leaf-watchers, they come up in the fall," or something a bit unfriendly such as, "There's such a thing as private property, you know." Instead, he simply asked me what I was looking for and wondered if he could help me out.

He could and did, as it turned out, but I was startled by his open, friendly approach and I missed much of what he said. My thoughts drifted back to conversations with friends in Boston who often referred to the Berkshires as "out west" or "Western Mass." Considering that Berkshire County is within

150 miles of Boston, it had always struck me as odd when people in the eastern part of the state made it sound as though places like Sheffield, Lee, and Williamstown were on the far side of the Mississippi River. When New Yorkers refer to the Berkshires as "up north," they imply a proximity with the Canadian border while in fact they are talking about a place within three hours of home.

The people, the landscape, and the mood of Berkshire County combine to create a sharp sense of separation from the rest of Massachusetts and New England. I have found myself expecting to see license plates on local cars bearing out-of-state insignia. I have been asked how things were back east, back in Massachusetts. While I have not discovered another state, exactly, I have found another state of mind. Even though I do not live in the county, I have come to think of it as an old friend, even-tempered and forgiving and always ready to welcome me, but it is still a long, long way from Back Bay to Becket, from Manhattan to Mount Washington.

Becket and Mount Washington are two of the thirty-two towns and cities that make up Berkshire County, the western-most county in Massachusetts. The county covers nearly 900 square miles and is flanked by Connecticut, New York, and Vermont. As the Taconic Range highlights the boundary between Berkshire and New York on the west, the Hoosac Range effectively separates the county from the rest of Massachusetts to the east. These ranges will not stop some of us from dreaming about the Rockies and the Alps, perhaps, but they do offer a pleasant alternative to the Adirondacks in New York and the White Mountains of New Hampshire, especially considering the extra time and energy it takes to get to these more renowned areas.

There are those, in fact, who would look down their noses at the Berkshires, claiming that they are actually hills, not mountains. They might even point out ambiguities such as

An Old Friend

the fact that the highest point in the town of Otis is known as Dorman Mountain (1956 feet) while the top of Savoy Mountain State Forest is called Spruce Hill (2566 feet). Do either of them qualify as mountains? Neither? Both? Does it make any difference? I suggest that those detractors who will not be happy until they find a true mountain—whatever that is—take their attitude right on up the highway with them and leave the rest of us alone to enjoy the year-round beauty of Berkshire County and its humble hilltops or soaring summits (take your pick).

There can be no debate on the matter of access to recreational areas in the Berkshires. Opportunities are nearly endless as some 15 percent of the acreage in the county is either public property or land owned by private, non-profit organizations which welcome the public.

The trails described in this book cross over many of these parcels of open land, but, of the tremendous amount of trails available, these make up only a sampling. I think the sampling is both thorough and representative and I invite you to use it as a recipe for exercise and exploration. Follow the example of any good cook by adding or substituting ingredients which will transform the essentials into a blend that is your own.

And if you need any advice along the way, just pull over to the side of the road and relax. Within a few minutes, I bet, that fellow pruning the bushes along his driveway is bound to wander over and ask if he can help you out.

Getting There

Automobile routes: From New York City, take the Taconic State Parkway north to Rte. 23 east or Interstate 90 (Mass. Pike Extension) east to exits at West Stockbridge and Lee.

From Boston, take either Rte. 2 west to the northern portion of the county, or Interstate 90 (Mass. Pike) west for the southern and central parts of the county.

From Albany, take Rte. 2 east to Williamstown and North Adams, or Interstate 90 east to exits at West Stockbridge and Lee.

From Springfield, take Interstate 90 (Mass. Pike) west to Lee or West Stockbridge, or take Interstate 91 north to Northampton and then take Rte. 9 West.

From Connecticut, take Rtes. 7 north, 8 north, or Interstate 91 north. If you choose I-91, turn to the west at Springfield onto the Mass. Pike or at Northampton onto Rte. 9.

Bus Lines: Service from New York City by Bonanza, Greyhound, and Vermont Transit; service from Boston by Bonanza and Greyhound; service from Albany by Arrow Line, Bonanza, and Greyhound; service from Springfield by Bonanza; service from Hartford and New Haven by Arrow Line.

Airlines: The only regularly scheduled air service is between New York and Pittsfield on Command Airways.

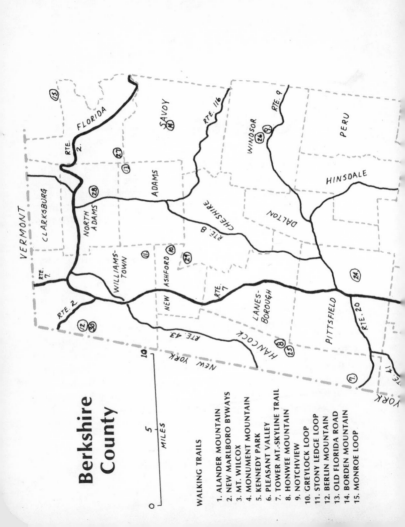

Berkshire County

WALKING TRAILS

1. ALANDER MOUNTAIN
2. NEW MARLBORO BYWAYS
3. MT. WILCOX
4. MONUMENT MOUNTAIN
5. KENNEDY PARK
6. PLEASANT VALLEY
7. TOWER MT.-SKYLINE TRAIL
8. HONWEE MOUNTAIN
9. NOTCHVIEW
10. GREYLOCK LOOP
11. STONY LEDGE LOOP
12. BERLIN MOUNTAIN
13. OLD FLORIDA ROAD
14. BORDEN MOUNTAIN
15. MONROE LOOP

MILES

0   5   10

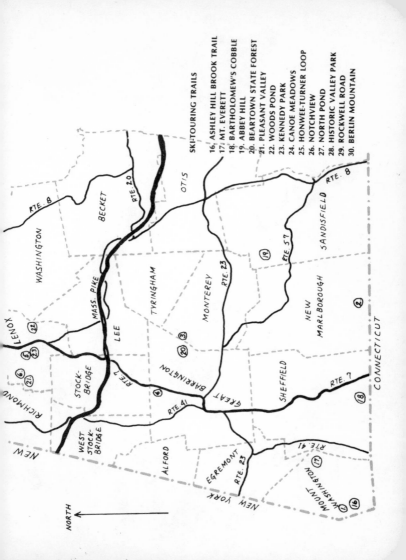

SKI-TOURING TRAILS

16. ASHLEY HILL BROOK TRAIL
17. MT. EVERETT
18. BARTHOLOMEW'S COBBLE
19. ABBEY HILL
20. BEARTOWN STATE FOREST
21. PLEASANT VALLEY
22. WOODS POND
23. KENNEDY PARK
24. CANOE MEADOWS
25. HONWEE-TURNER LOOP
26. NOTCHVIEW
27. NORTH POND
28. HISTORIC VALLEY PARK
29. ROCKWELL ROAD
30. BERLIN MOUNTAIN

NORTH

Geology

Some like nothing better than to lie on a lawn or beach on a warm summer's night and stare out into the heavens, whether or not they know a planet from a satellite. There is an attraction in that limitless expanse that fixes them and they laugh at the thought of infinity. Others must know where they are at all times; they get uneasy when their eye wanders ahead of the next few steps, and they get the chills when they try to imagine what is out there behind Jupiter.

As they gaze back through hundreds of millions of years trying to piece together the puzzle of the creation and development of the earth, geologists must stumble frequently. They must realize that sometimes they will never know, and they must be ready to admit that a process that they think they have identified could have happened 50 to 200 million years back. It does not sound very scientific, but when dealing with time spans that great, who cares about twenty million years here, 50 million there?

Between two and five million years ago, Berkshire County and the rest of western New England was conceived when the furnace at the earth's core overheated and caused stretching and compressing on the surface of the planet. Under the Berkshires and the Green Mountains to the north, great infusions of molten rock pushed up under the bedrock crust with such force that the crust finally let go. When it did, it was thrown up out of the sea then covering the area to make islands—islands that were dominated by towering rocky summits. Some tens of millions of years after this initial stage of land building, the range we now call the Taconics slid off this massive ridge, probably because the underpinning along the western slope shifted or gave way.

Before the mountains could wipe the sweat from their eyes, they were subjected to atmospheric forces that were as determined to destroy them as the heat had been to create them. Wind, water, and cold temperatures were the chief culprits. The wind dusted from the surface anything it could carry. Water found its way everywhere—here to sweep away dirt and gravel; there to wait until winter when it froze and chipped off large pieces of rock that tumbled down to stream beds to be ground down at the water's leisure during the spring and summer. The process took awhile, of course, but then there was no hurry; millions, even hundreds of millions, of years were at hand. However long it took, the job was eventually completed and the lofty mountains were reduced to nearly flat plain except for a few especially resistant outcroppings such as Mt. Greylock. Rivers that once ran wild, tearing away at the uplands, became languid wanderers.

There were perhaps several cycles of mountain building and erosion along this pattern. Eventually, the forces that caused this type of construction quieted, but the surface of the land was not still as more subtle forces went to work. The earth was settling and had not found its balance—as it has not yet. Cycles of uplifting and erosion continued, but this time the uplifting was in the form of gentle swellings here and there. Geologists believe that at one time the entire area was lifted up, pretty much intact, some two thousand feet and tilted slightly towards the present New England coastline so that the nearly dead rivers once again found a reason to ramble and carry away anything that was not too hard or heavy. The flat area that had been left after earlier cycles of erosion was now chipped and sliced into something that approximated the present lay of the land. The last of these gentle upwellings occurred somewhere around ten million years ago. Since then there have been no major land-building stages, although constant erosion has continued to refine the topography.

Erosion was sped up about a million years ago when there was a climatic change over the northern hemisphere. Gradually the temperature dropped until it was, on an annual average, a few degrees cooler—enough to extend the winters and cause an increase in precipitation and erosion in north temperate zones. Far to the north a process was begun that was to have an enormous impact on the region. Snow began to fall in arctic regions with increased intensity, and, because the summers were now cooler and shorter, the snow did not melt as quickly or thoroughly as it had earlier. Soon there was snow on the ground year-round and more was added to it with every period of precipitation. The snow layers increased steadily until, finally, the weight of the upper layers became too much for the lower layers to bear. The snow near ground level was compressed into ice and eventually began to ooze out towards the south. An enormous mound of snow had become a glacier.

The creeping river of ice gradually picked up speed as the snow kept falling in the north, adding bulk and force to the infant glacier. The glacier's initial movements were tentative and its dimenions measurable. But as the snows continued to pile up in the north, new fuel was added to the fire and soon the glacier had traveled far from its source and had grown to proportions hard to imagine. Picture a layer of ice thousands of feet thick lying over the entire Northeast and a good deal of the upper Midwest as well.

As the ice made its way into southern New England, it followed the most inviting routes—the river valleys. Because

Berkshire County is bordered on the north by the Green Mountains, on the east by the Hoosac Range, and on the west by the Taconics, it is likely that the ice did not enter the area until well after it filled the adjacent Connecticut and Hudson river valleys. Fingers of ice probably first crept into the county through the Hoosac River Valley where it passes out of the county at Williamstown and where the north fork of the Hoosac makes its way into the county at Clarksburg. Eventually the ice built up to such a depth that even the mountain barriers could not hold it back; later invasions spilled over the gaps in the Hoosacs and the Taconics.

At first only the valleys were covered with ice, but gradually the entire region filled up until even the highest peaks were buried, and there was silence in Berkshire County and all of New England. The only signs of life were the eerie creeping of the ice and occasional rumblings as chunks of ice ground against one another, trying to find comfortable resting spots for the duration of the siege. They did not rest for long, however, as the force of weight from the north constantly dispatched late model chunks to replace or reinforce those that had gone before.

As the ice passed over New England it dislodged anything that was not securely moored; it scooped up giant boulders and acres of topsoil with an ease that would leave the operators of modern earth-moving machines shaking their heads in wonder. Most animals, of course, had gotten the message from the cooling temperatures in time to head south well in advance of the glacier's arrival, but plant life that had held on in the face of torturous frosts and snow squalls was obliterated immediately.

When the ice finally reached the lead edge of the glacier, it succumbed to warmer temperatures and melted; but even as one chunk released its load of rocky rubble, another appeared from under the mantle to take its place in the sun and, in time, melt. When the glacier's forward movement was stopped and its leading edge was stationary for a few hundred years, piles of rock and gravel—called moraines—built up until they were sizable enough to deserve names, like Cape Cod and Long Island.

From the layering of deposits in moraines, geologists have determined that the ice sheet came and went several times before it finally receded for good—we hope—around twelve thousand years ago. The face of New England must have been as raw and unattractive as that of a river valley after a flood. But gradually life returned on the wings of the south wind, and before long hearty plants and animals established a foothold and worked the land until their more delicate relatives found the region habitable. Erosion got back to work after its long respite to sculpt and buff the landscape into a kinder form.

The years have erased most of the glacier's topographical rearranging from view, although the expert can find traces still with a minimal amount of digging. Luckily even the uninformed can find evidence of the ice if he just knows where to look. Probably the most spectacular example of the glacier's presence in Berkshire County is the Hopper, a cirque on the west face of the Mt. Greylock chain. Cirques were formed by small independent glaciers that preceded the arrival of the main sheet and lingered on after it left. As snow accumulated at the top of the mountain, it pushed the ice beneath it down to lower elevations where it melted and gradually eroded the topsoil, then infiltrated the bedrock and froze and chipped off chunks of rock which tumbled to the valley bottom. The process of erosion and undermining continued for hundreds of years until, finally, a deep, steep-sided bowl was formed where there had once been a solid mountain.

Moraines made by the remnants of the glaciers in valley bottoms formed earthen dams which backed up streams to form some of the ponds and lakes in the Berkshires. And many of the smaller, flatter hills—called drumlins—may have been formed by the ice sheet as it compacted fine sediments into layers that built up into a hill. But probably the most evident feature of the glacier's work is the scattering of rocks and boulders of every size and description everywhere across the Berkshire landscape. Today they are considered picturesque, but the early settlers must have been dismayed at the litter of rocks that slowed their efforts to clear land for cultivation. As God-fearing as they were, they must have cursed some power up there or down there, especially since they did not know how the rocks had gotten there in the first place. As late as the mid-nineteenth century, some geologists believed that the rocks had been washed over New England by Noah's flood.

It took the imagination of the romantic poets of England and our own Thoreau and Emerson to discover the beauty in what had been considered a rugged, hostile environment. The old-timers had neither the time nor the inclination to look on the steep, rocky hills with anything but frustration. Even after farmers had cleared the rocks from the surface of the fields and piled them into the stone walls that crisscross the woods today, they had to contend with a new rock crop every spring as frost and the plow brought another batch to the surface. Those pioneers would surely have scratched their heads when told that one day there would be areas in New England that would run out of rocks, and that people would pay good money to buy enough to fashion a stone wall around their yards when they had nothing to fence in or out—except maybe the eyes of their neighbors.

Those same pioneers considered the hills themselves to be intimidating enough so that Berkshire County was not settled until well after neighboring areas. They referred to the Hoosac Range as the Berkshire Barrier, and when they finally did push over into the valley, they saw it as a harsh and inhospitable environment; they knew they were in for a never-

Geology

ending struggle if they attempted to tame it. The soil turned out to be fine for farming, but the glacier had not left much of it in any one place. Cultivation was at best difficult as fields had to be carved out of the rock-strewn hillsides that might be stripped of their covering come the next downpour.

Berkshire's main drawing card in the settlers' eyes was the abundance of moving water. You cannot go more than a mile or two in any direction without running across a brook, stream, or river. The principal rivers are the Housatonic and the Hoosac (spelled Hoosic on some maps). The headwaters of the Housatonic merge just south of the center of modern Pittsfield and meander down through the south county towns of Lenox, Lee, Stockbridge, Great Barrington, and Sheffield, on into Connecticut and finally to Long Island Sound. The south branch of the Hoosac starts off from Cheshire Reservoir (also known as Hoosac Lake) and heads north through Adams to North Adams, joining the north branch which starts over the Vermont border north of Clarksburg. From North Adams the Hoosac heads west and passes through Williamstown and the southwest corner of Vermont until it crosses into New York State and finally empties into the Hudson about twenty miles north of Albany.

All sorts of smaller streams, from dribbling creeks to tumbling mountain brooks, feed these two major rivers or wander out of the county on their own. Where streams pass over hard bedrock, they usually move quickly in tight, steep channels; where they find areas of softer sedimentary rock, such as limestone, they create wide flat valleys through which they meander at an easy pace. Gently or ferociously, these rivers and streams will, given enough time, wear away anything near them until Berkshire County is once again reduced to a nearly flat area, bare of her most attractive features, the hills.

History

As English, French, and Dutch outposts slowly spread up and down the Atlantic coastline during the seventeenth century, settlement of the interior regions lagged behind. Settlers were not anxious to remove themselves from the lifeline to the homeland, the sea. Also, the interior looked dark and forbidding, clothed as it was in almost impenetrable forests and supposedly overrun with Indians who were imagined to be hostile, and in some cases were.

Eventually, however, when the outposts grew into towns and became more secure, curiosity and dreams of riches persuaded some daring souls to leave the longshore sanctuaries and explore the interior. At first they explored the major rivers of the area, such as the Hudson and the Connecticut, where they were able to sail a good distance upriver before they ran into navigation problems. While the headwaters of the Housatonic reach well into Berkshire County, the river is narrow and is interrupted by natural obstructions near its mouth. So the way into Berkshire for the white man was not to be by water. He would have to find his way over either the Hoosac Range—the Berkshire Barrier—on the eastern border of the region or the Taconics on the west, not an inviting prospect in either case. While we whistle over these hills with ease today, they must have looked like giant impediments back in those days, the more so since the colonists did not know what lay beyond the mountains. They were fairly sure that there were Indians in the region and they were fairly sure that that meant trouble.

By the middle of the seventeenth century, settlements bustled along the Connecticut and Hudson rivers but the area between them—the valleys of the Housatonic and the Hoosac and the hills that flank them—remained a wilderness. The area was visited now and again by trappers and lone explorers, but they left no records of their visits. The first recorded excursion into what was to become Berkshire County took place in 1676 when a detachment of English colonists from Westfield crossed over the Berkshire Barrier in pursuit of a band of Indians who had been raiding settlements along the Connecticut River. The soldiers, led by Major John Talcott, caught up with the Indians at an encampment alongside a river—the Housatonic. Here the English attacked the Indians and drove off those that they did not kill. The survivors headed west, presumably to join up with the main body of the Mohicans in the Hudson River Valley. Talcott's party headed back to Westfield having learned very little about the area they had just been in. The Berkshire region remained a mystery.

Although the colonists living on the banks of the Connecticut did not know it at the time, the land over the mountains was relatively empty. The Mohawks and other members of the Iroquois Confederacy were largely content to stay on the west side of the Hudson. The more peaceful Algonquin, who occupied much of southern New England, shied away from the Berkshire area perhaps because they were happy to have a buffer zone between them and the quarrelsome, often violent, Mohawks. Also, there was not much pressure to occupy every valley since in all of New England there were only about ten thousand Indians. They frequented those areas that were most accessible to their migration routes. In the winter they moved south to the shores of Long Island Sound where there was less snow and cold and where they lived off shellfish. Hunting parties stayed in the north for a while longer, but rarely through the entire winter. In spring they moved back inland to catch shad and salmon in their annual spawning runs and to plant corn and squashes. They burned off sections of the underbrush here and there to fertilize the soil and to make it easier to pursue deer and other game.

The Algonquin lived in small groups of six or eight wigwams and only became attached to specific locations when nature proved particularly bountiful. Otherwise they were not territorial and only clashed with the colonists when they felt they had been pushed too far or treated unfairly. Perhaps they would not have been as submissive if they had known the intentions of the white man, who was, in fact, invading their land and pushing them back further and further into the interior, offering only a few baubles and jugs of rum in return for lands that would eventually stretch across the continent.

While it is probable that there were some Indian encampments in Berkshire before 1600, there is no hard evidence to prove it. The first white men to enter the county were probably Dutchmen coming over the Taconics from their trading post at Fort Orange (now Albany) established in 1624. Henry Hudson had sailed the river he named for himself as far as the rapids north of Albany in 1609 looking for the elusive Northwest Passage to the Orient. He was unsuccessful, of course, but he did establish for the Dutch a foothold in the new world which was formalized with the founding of the Dutch West India Company in 1621. Fur trading was the economic backbone of the colony, and it was not long before some of the Dutch themselves went into the wilderness to trap, having learned the trade from the Indians.

Soon enough some of the Dutch introduced the Indians to a concept that was new to the natives—private ownership of land. In return for meaningless paper money and other European inventions, the Indians agreed to let the Dutch build cabins here and there. Most likely the Indians had no idea of what the Dutch were up to. And the Dutch could hardly expect the Indians to guarantee their rights when the Indians were mystified by the deeds the foreigners drew up to prove ownership. Those same deeds were meaningless for the Dutch as well, it turned out, since a few cabins in the wilderness did not represent a population large enough to maintain a settlement.

By 1700, the Dutch presence in Berkshire was great enough to impress English colonists in Massachusetts that, if they ever wanted to lay claim to the area, they had better get on with it. The Dutch had neither the manpower nor the determination to settle the region, but Berkshire would probably have become theirs and eventually part of New York State by default if the English made no effort to settle it themselves.

In 1722, Joseph Parsons of Westfield and Thomas Nash of Northampton were granted petitions to settle in southern Berkshire by the Massachusetts General Court. The petitioners agreed to support a school and a church and had to pay a pittance to the court for an enormous chunk of land. This money was passed on to the Algonquin Chief Konkapot in 1724 as compensation for what turned out be about one-third of Berkshire County as it stands today. The exact amount paid to Konkapot was "460 (British) pounds, 3 barrels of sider (sic) and 30 quarts of rum." If the chief had had any idea of what he was in for, he surely would have offered token resistance or at least demanded a higher price.

The intentions of the earliest setters—led by Matthew Noble in 1725—were reasonable: they meant to coexist with the Indians as far as was possible and they encouraged the establishment of missions from the outset. The desire to Christianize the "heathen" was as strong as the desire to make the peaceful natives of the Housatonic Valley allies against the still hostile Mohawks to the north. Of course, the Indians were probably not the best of students; they must have been puzzled by the new language they were expected to learn overnight, by the new religion, by the new laws and customs.

The colonists had rigid town plans in mind before they even arrived at an area they planned to settle. The plan called for a tight cluster of dwellings around a central meeting house which would also serve as a church. As fears of Indian raids waned, the communities began to spread out, at first to cultivate larger tracts of land and later because land in the outlying areas was cheaper. The local Indians never did understand what the white man was up to when it came to the use of land. Shortly after Sheffield became the first incorporated town in the area in 1733, Ephraim Williams, the patriarch of the family which has left a lasting legacy to Berkshire County including Williams College, persuaded a reluctant Dutch landowner to sell him some 290 acres. He immediately turned around and traded this parcel to the Indians in return for 4,000 acres about a dozen miles north of Sheffield. Surely the Indians were bewildered by this arrangement, but they did not have the power to stop it. Their confusion was probably not lessened until, fifty years later, they found themselves displaced to a reservation in western New York State, and later as far west as Wisconsin. So much for coexistence.

Settlement of the rest of the county, particularly the northern section, did not follow quickly on the heels of the incorporation of Sheffield. The area was still threatened by attack from the Mohawks, who by this time had allied themselves with the French who were contesting colonial supremacy with the English. In an effort to persuade those east of the Berkshire Barrier to leave their sanctuaries and head west, the General Court laid out another five townships in the county in 1735 as well as two (Charlemont and Colrain) along the Deerfield River Valley. The five in Berkshire were Becket, Tyringham, New Marlborough, and Sandisfield in the southeast corner of the county, and Pontoosuck, later known as Pittsfield, in the central section. A string of forts was built along the northern border of the state, stretching from Northfield to North Adams, the site of Fort Massachusetts. These were supposed to deter raids by the French and Indians and protect the settlers in the southern part of Berkshire as well as those along the Connecticut River.

Confidence in this line of defense was severely shaken in 1746, when a party of French and Indians attacked Fort Massachusetts, overwhelmed the defenders, and burned the fort to the ground. Settlers as far south as Sheffield felt the reverberations of this loss; they scurried to tighten up their communities, and some even took the opportunity to head back to the safety of the Connecticut River Valley. The Indian threat to settlement in Berkshire County lasted until 1761 when the French and Indian War finally ended. From that point on, the rate of settlement increased dramatically. Only a year later, in 1762, the General Court auctioned off lands which were eventually incorporated into the present towns of Richmond, Lenox, Savoy, Windsor, Adams, Hinsdale, and Peru. The colony was happy to accommodate the land greed that possessed many of the settlers. Those who invested in the new area of the county saw large profits as their reward, and the colony profited from taxes levied on the holdings. Every new settlement reinforced Massachusetts' claim to the land as part of the colony, almost a foregone conclusion by this time. Still, land claims between rival colonies were continuing, and the General Court was anxious to preempt any new challenge to Massachusetts' claim to Berkshire County.

Many of the proprietors who bid and won at the auction of the General Court never settled in Berkshire. They were content to stay in eastern Massachusetts hoping, of course, that their investments would pay off, but not so desperate that they felt the need to actually travel to or work the land they had purchased. At times, residents of newly incorporated towns had to petition the court to make the proprietors comply with the conditions of their purchase. From an early date, settlers realized that they had to make do for themselves, that neither the proprietors nor the General Court was going to pave the way to an easy life in the new county. This led to a feeling of separation from the rest of the state that still exists today; it also made for a frontier attitude of independence and self-sufficiency that one would have expected to find in far more remote areas of the colonies. But Berkshire, owing to its late start in settlement, resembled frontier areas farther afield.

Until the end of the French and Indian hostilities, settlers moving into Berkshire were almost exclusively from the eastern part of Massachusetts. The last part of the eighteenth century, however, saw ever-increasing numbers of newcomers from other colonies, principally from Connecticut. They came for the same reasons that had prompted their predecessors: they found religious conditions intolerable in their first home, or they felt that the economic opportunities in the newly settled area were more promising. The decision to leave home and settle a new area cannot have been an easy one. Richard Birdsall, in his excellent book of 1959 entitled *Berkshire County, A Cultural History,* quotes from a letter written in 1773 by Joseph Bennet, a founder of Cheshire:

> We have not only had to endure the scoffs, flouts, and reproaches of the part of the people we moved from among, but we had the sympathy of sorrow and affection, on the other part add to this our coming such a long and tedious journey through so many difficulties that attended it, into a wilderness country and

29

there set down without either friend or neighbor anigh us and to undergo all hardships that befell us, bear them we must for we have nowhere to go for relief. Thus by our own hardships, frugality and industry we were the first that brought forward this place.

Nevertheless, settlement of the county proceeded at a steady rate. During the Revolution it dwindled dramatically, only to bounce back again at the conclusion of the war. By 1780, it is estimated that there were 30,000 inhabitants in the county, or almost 400 to the square mile.

While the Revolution was not fought on Berkshire soil, the residents knew that it was fought for Berkshire soil, and for their right to determine for themselves how they wished to live. Within three days of Paul Revere's ride to Lexington and Concord, two regiments of Berkshire's finest were marching east to help out against the British. As early as July of 1774, in fact, a convention of Berkshire County residents met at the Red Lion Inn in Stockbridge to discuss the intolerable situation to the east where the Massachusetts charter had been revoked and the port of Boston closed. The convention quickly adopted what has since been called the "First Declaration of Independence." The Berkshirites were not merely whistling in the dark; their defiance of the crown was real enough to prompt the governor of the colony, Thomas Gage, to write back to England: "A flame sprang up at the end of the Province. The popular rage is very high in Berkshire and makes its way rapidly to the East."

On May 10, 1775, only three weeks after the battles of Lexington and Concord, Ethan Allen and his Green Mountain Boys (who included in their ranks a good many Berkshire Mountain boys) took Ticonderoga and Crown Point from the British without a fight. It was over two years later that men of local militia were able to see some direct action. While their neighbors and kinfolk who were regulars were seeing all kinds of action with Washington's army, the local militia was left to take care of things at home. That amounted to overtime work in the fields and the forests to keep the communities functioning, but it did not include any fighting. So by the time the call went out for any able-bodied men to come to Bennington to try to stop Burgoyne's advance, anyone who could walk dropped his pitchfork and ran north with a gun slung over his shoulder. Even a man of the cloth, the Reverend Thomas Allen of Pittsfield, dropped his ministerial duties long enough to scurry up over the Vermont border to help defeat Burgoyne in the critical battle at Bennington.

With the end of the Revolution, Berkshire residents could get back to the welcome, if sometimes tedious, job of working the land and building up the communities which they now felt were really theirs. There was a slight interruption of this domesticity in the winter of 1786-87 — Shays' Rebellion, manned by veterans of the war, mostly farmers, who felt that they had not been adequately compensated for their military service. In order to keep their homesteads afloat while they were off fighting, the veterans had had to go into debt, and these debts were not easy to pay off when they returned home to find even heavier taxes levied by the state. Arms were taken up, but the fighting never became very serious; those assigned the task of putting down the rebellion were often friends and neighbors of the rebels and, in a good many cases, sympathized with them, the common enemy being the state government in Boston. Few lives were lost on either side, but the rebels got their point across, and, under a provision of the Federal Constitution of 1787, they were paid for time spent in the Continental Army.

Towards the end of the eighteenth century, agricultural self-sufficiency continued to be the main goal of Berkshire citizens. But with improved roads and continuing immigration the county was full in terms of agricultural development. It was not long before some of Berkshire's native sons started to move north and west, sometimes enticed by the wide open spaces and promise of riches and sometimes driven from the county by the depressing prospect of scratching against its harsh physical realities—the rocky hillsides and shallow layers of topsoil—with no great reward in the offing. The prime real estate by this time had been taken up, and what was left had been clear cut in many areas for firewood and pasturage. While most of the farmers did make a go of it, they did not practice far-sighted agricultural techniques. Very little thought was given to conserving or replenishing valuable resources, probably in part because of the idea that there was a boundless supply, if not in Berkshire, then farther west and north.

Very early on, settlers seemed determined to cut down as much of the primeval forest as they could. Of course they needed the wood and the open spaces, but determination to clear the land must also have been at least an unconscious response to Berkshire as it was first seen by white men—as something like a temperate jungle. A parallel phenomenon exists today where land developers are apt to bulldoze anything that stands in order to facilitate the building of roads and, later, houses. Then, after selling off the lots or the homes, the developer takes the money and heads south leaving a bald landscape. After a few years, seedlings begin to appear in front of most houses, but it will take awhile for these to mature and offer any real privacy or protection from the elements. Early illustrations of Berkshire County are remarkable for the lack of trees near buildings; the settlers left nothing for an Indian to hide behind, nothing to remind them of the wilderness that they had struggled to tame. And they were too busy simply keeping themselves alive (and adhering to the strict Puritan code) to think in terms of beautification.

By the beginning of the nineteenth century the original town proprietors (who owned the largest tracts of land) and lawyers had joined the ministers as the most important men in any town. Everybody else farmed—usually on their own land—or worked at supplying the farmers' needs or processing what the farmers produced. A typical town had at least one gristmill, as many sawmills as there were brooks to power them, a tannery, a mine if any iron had been found, and possibly a forge and a marble quarry.

It was not long before the local mills, forges, and tanneries were being called factories. The introduction of machinery in the early nineteenth century made the local enterprises so efficient that they were soon producing more goods than the local inhabitants could use. Simultaneously, a network of new stage routes was spreading through the area, so that it became possible to export the surplus. These new roads were called turnpikes; they were built by private contractors who charged a toll for their use. Soon after the turn of the century these roads saw a steady flow of stage traffic, carrying both passengers and freight, between towns in the Berkshires and cities such as Hudson and Albany, New York, and Hartford, Connecticut.

The Berkshire economy, while still essentially agrarian, was gradually becoming industrialized. Where at one time attitudes and ideas had been centered around the local church and town hall, now the attention of Berkshire residents was being distracted by the lure of profits to be made trading with the outside world. Most of the industry gravitated toward the towns bordering the larger rivers, especially the Housatonic and the Hoosac, since the increased demand required larger factories which in turn needed more water power. The one man or one family milling operations along smaller streams in the hill towns began to die off and with them the self-sufficiency that had characterized Berkshire life in the century since the first settlers had come into the county. While the first settlers had been so strapped that they found it difficult to support their local minister (a legal obligation), their descendants were now doing well enough to support schools and libraries. Williams College, which opened in 1793, quickly became a focus for support and pride within the county.

The newfound wealth that was being enjoyed by Berkshire industrialists was based principally on the export of marble, iron, wool, and paper. In 1801, Zenas Crane started a paper mill in Dalton that still bears his name and which still makes some of the highest grade of paper to be found, including some that is used by the U.S. Treasury for currency. While the Crane company was the first and one of the few surviving today, it was not alone for long; by the end of the Civil War there were twenty-eight paper mills spread along the Housatonic River north of the Connecticut border. Marble quarries and works were to be found in almost every Berkshire town, and the quality of the marble was so high that it was used for buildings in most cities along the eastern seaboard. Textile mills cropped up along the Hoosac and the Housatonic, and Berkshire was recognized as a prime area of production. While the mills were at first dependent on local wool, it was not long before the demand exceeded the supply and wool had to be imported. Factories producing glass, potash, seed oils, leather, and rope sprung up along the rivers, but it was eventually the production of iron that took over as the dominant industry in the area. The existence of rich deposits of iron ore had long been known, but methods of extracting and refining it remained primitive until late in the eighteenth century, and not until the railroads offered a practical means of transportation did the industry really take off.

By the mid-nineteenth century there were some two dozen blast furnaces in Berkshire County, all requiring a tremendous amount of charcoal to smelt the ore. And finally, to complete the industrialization of the area, the railroads began to appear. Now the factories had a quick and dependable means of exporting their goods. In 1838, the railroad spanned the Taconics from Hudson to West Stockbridge. From the east came tracks from Springfield to Pittsfield and on through to Albany in 1841. And a system which followed the Housatonic from the Connecticut shoreline to Great Barrington was completed in 1843. Three years later a spur was run from Pittsfield to North Adams, finally linking up the whole county with a rail system. With the railroads came the final, vital ingredient to successful industrialization. Chard Powers Smith, in *The Housatonic, Puritan River* (New York, 1946), describes the transformed scene in the northern reaches of the valley, including two-thirds of Berkshire County: ". . . the marble quarries kept parts of the town mantled under white dust, while the racket of sawing and blasting mingled with that of the trains to whose sidings the carts creaked with the big slabs."

Of more lasting impact was the iron industry, and here again C.P. Smith paints a telling picture:

Though the furnaces were partially housed, still the great stone stacks gave up to the sky an occasional burst of glow, and the breasts of molten metal a sharper glare, while the leather bellows on beam frames violated the echoes twenty-four hours a day with animal-like growls and groans audible up to five miles. To serve the furnaces and forges, virtually every mountain of Berkshires and the Litchfield Hills smoked with charcoal piles, and through the years the shorn wastes where the forest had been grew up their sides to the summits. As from the original hilltop farms, the uncovered soil ran off the rocks, leaving the granite hills of New England more naked than ever.

Once again, the Berkshire folk had gone overboard in their efforts to secure for themselves a better way of life, caring little for the waste that they were creating, not taking the time to consider what damage they were doing and what the future might bring.

By the tail end of the century, cheaper and more available raw materials were harvested in other parts of the country. Berkshire had enjoyed a period of prosperity that she would never regain, nor could she regain the simple, tidy self-sufficiency of the colonial and revolutionary periods. Before the prosperity petered out, however, it was left to the building of the Hoosac Tunnel, a monumental undertaking, to punctuate the period of industrial prosperity as nothing before had.

While the southern part of the county had prospered from as early on as 1800, the northern section lagged behind, owing largely to the increased distances to market. Although the railroad had reached all the way up to North Adams in 1846, it was a long journey down the county and then on to the big cities south and west. The towns of Adams and North Adams, both situated on the banks of the powerful Hoosac River, wanted more direct access to the outside world, especially east and west. And the powers that be in Boston felt strongly that a northern route across the state and into New York would do wonders for the economy of the region and for the reputation of the state as an industrial power. These attitudes were born out of a spirit of desperation, as competition from the west was growing stronger all the time. Although many thought the drilling of the tunnel a supreme folly, it made better sense than another idea that had been put forward. Some thought a canal was the best way through the mountains. Surely they had not considered the obstacles inherent in such a project, but the idea was advanced nevertheless.

At any rate, in 1848 the Troy and Greenfield Railroad Company secured a charter for the building of a tunnel that was to be four and three-quarter miles long and, at its deepest, something over one thousand feet below ground level. From each end, workers started chipping away at the granite with hand tools and black powder explosives. A shaft was sunk at the center of the tunnel and workers were lowered down to dig out from the middle to join those who were working in from each end. Machines were developed to help the digging process, but they were largely ineffective, and progress had to rely on the awesome slowness of chipping away with hand-held augurs and hand-swung sledge hammers. The black powder detonations made for tremendous rumbles in the shaft and for great billows of noxious smoke, but they did not make much of an impact on the stubborn mountain. Finally, with the development of nitroglycerin, work sped up a bit, but not without an increased number of casualties among the work force owing to the extremely volatile nature of the explosive. By chance it was discovered that the nitro was stable when frozen, and thereafter it was always transported under mounds of ice. Finally, at a cost of 195 lives, 24 years, and $15 million, the Hoosac Tunnel was opened to rail service in the winter of 1875, at the time the longest tunnel on the continent. North Adams immediately became something of a boom town, catching up quickly with the prosperity enjoyed in the southern part of the county.

Now the entire county was well connected in all directions and changed forever. Like it or not, Berkshire had caught up with and was very much a part of the nineteenth century. Meanwhile, with a lot less noise but no less energy, there had been developed in the parlors and studies of south-central Berkshire a movement that would eventually rival the notoriety of the industrial boom. The new commodity was literature, in some cases less negotiable than the material goods coming out of factories and mines, but certainly as significant.

William Cullen Bryant was born in Cummington in 1794. By 1820, he was known in literary circles in Boston and New York as a first-rate poet—many thought him America's best.

It was a shock to some that he devoted most of his energy to the glorification of nature and not to God, and he even had the audacity to praise and revere the American Indian for his appreciation and knowledge of the natural world. Because he was unable to support himself with his writing, Bryant worked as a lawyer in Great Barrington from 1816 through 1825, but the law did not suit him and he moved to New York to work on a small periodical. He eventually became the editor of the *Evening Post* in New York and is remembered as a great journalist as well as a poet. He did not write much poetry after he moved to New York, but his early poems left a lasting mark and served as an introduction to outsiders of the natural beauty and heritage of Berkshire County. One of the few locals who saw his genius early on was Catherine Sedgwick, who became a best-selling author in 1822 with the publication of *A New England Tale*. Her contribution to literature in the nineteenth century, however, was in some ways less tangible than the books she authored. She was best known to the literary luminaries as a friend and supporter of those around her whom she identified as having genius. At various times, she and her brothers entertained and encouraged Bryant, Oliver Wendell Holmes, Henry Wadsworth Longfellow, Nathaniel Hawthorne, and Herman Melville, all of whom spent time in the Berkshires during mid-century.

Longfellow visited the Berkshires often during the forties but was never quite comfortable. Perhaps, on the other hand, he was too comfortable, since he continually complained that the mountains made him drowsy and unable to get much work done. He had grown up around Boston and missed the sea, and remarked that he wished he could blend the two environments somehow. Although he owned a large piece of land on the Housatonic, he never spent the year through in the Berkshires.

Oliver Wendell Holmes was another seasonal visitor to the Berkshires, staying at his family place in Pittsfield for the summers 1849-56. While his roots were in Boston, he took to the Berkshires without hesitation, and filled his poems with Berkshire details. He wrote several to commemorate specific public occasions.

In 1850, both Herman Melville and Nathaniel Hawthorne moved to Berkshire County. Both had spent some time in the area in the late thirties, but since then they had been on or near the sea. Hawthorne, fresh off the successful publication of *The Scarlet Letter*, moved to a small cottage in Lenox equipped with the material that would a year later see the light as *The House of the Seven Gables*. Melville moved into an old family house in Pittsfield, bringing with him a head full of *Moby Dick*. Both books were written while the respective authors were in the Berkshires, but neither, of course, drew on local material. Hawthorne and Melville met for the first time in the summer of 1850, and for a short while were extremely close. Melville, in fact, felt that, had it not been for the delight he derived from his relationship with Hawthorne, he might not have been able to see his way through the trying exercise of writing *Moby Dick*. *The House of the Seven Gables* came a bit easier to Hawthorne, but there is no question that he found Melville a sympathetic and encouraging colleague. Hawthorne, a shy man given to depression, reveled in the atmosphere of Lenox for a while, but it was not long before he felt the urge to move on, prompted by the unpredictable and harsh winters and by his fame which drew curious stargazers to his door. He left Lenox in late 1851.

Melville stayed on for another dozen years, trying to salvage his literary reputation which took a severe beating when *Moby Dick* was given little notice by the critics and the public. He was seen by his neighbors as a distant, impious man, but he did not seem to care about his social reputation. When he was accused of being eccentric and maybe a bit insane, he was apt to agree. He occupied himself with his writing, with a little farming and with roaming the Berkshire Hills on foot. In 1863, he moved to New York where he supported himself working as a customs official. Fame came to him only after his death.

While the literary notoriety had peaked, industry boomed along at an accelerating pace. Men and material were diverted to the Civil War cause in the early sixties, but were soon back on track after the defeat of the South. Railroads now crisscrossed the nation and new inventions were daily revolutionizing industry. Fortunes were made almost overnight during the industrial revolution, and it was not long before Berkshire felt the effect of some of these fortunes in the birth of a new industry. A few people made so many untaxed millions that they had a full-time job just to spend them. For some reason, Lenox and surrounding southern Berkshire towns caught the fancy of a few of the earliest millionaires who started to build "cottages" in the area. These were second, and in some cases, third and fourth homes. Probably the owner had a house in New York, maybe one also in the South and one in Europe as well. An average cottage was situated on top of a hill surrounded by hundreds of acres, many of them in gardens and lawns, had thirty to forty rooms, and was built and decorated in some highly ornate and imitative style. Building materials, servants, and art treasures were imported from Europe. Of course local materials and manpower were employed as well, and toward the tail end of the century, when local industries were starting to fail, the resort industry employed many of those who would have gone without work. Enormous hotels were built to accommodate those who could not afford to compete with the cottage builders but who felt it necessary to rub shoulders with them.

The "cottage" industry peaked right around the turn of the twentieth century, but began to fade fairly soon afterwards. The ratification of the sixteenth amendment (tax on income) did not help, nor did the First World War. There was a mild revival during the twenties, but that was quashed for good by the crash of the stock market in 1929. Some of the cottages burned down, some rotted, and others were donated for use as schools. Very few remained in private hands during or after the depression. The era when southern Berkshire was a playground for the superrich had passed as the agricultural and industrial eras had passed before. But the reputation of Berkshire County as a lovely, accessible resort area was established for good, and is alive and well today.

Natural History

In the south, the Berkshires begin as a green ripple in the stony landscape of northwest Connecticut. This rolled up portion of the Appalachians, called the Litchfield Hills, becomes Connecticut's last claim to wilderness at Bear Mountain whose northern flanks reach into Massachusetts, hard on the New York border. In Massachusetts, the ripple broadens into a region of wind-swept mountains, deep ravines, steep cliffs, waterfalls, high pastures, and bogs with plant life like that of the Canadian tundra. The range ends abruptly at Jug End near Egremont, and the land becomes more open and rolling throughout. Only Mt. Wilcox in Beartown State Forest and October Mountain between Great Barrington and Pittsfield mirror the roughness of the land just north of the Connecticut border where Mt. Everett (2600 feet) and Mt. Frissel (2450 feet), both in the Taconic Range, are high country companions. The Taconics on the west are paralleled by the southern extension of the Hoosac Range—the Berkshire Barrier—on the east; between the two lies the flat valley of the Housatonic River.

North of Pittsfield, the Barrier continues along the eastern boundary of the county, gradually rising in elevation towards the north. Similarly, the Taconics take on added height as they straddle the New York border on their way into Vermont. The Hoosac River, running north and eventually west from Cheshire, separates the two ranges. Mt. Greylock (3491 feet) and its neighbors—Saddle Ball Mountain, Mt. Fitch, Mt. Williams, and Mt. Prospect—dominate the skyline of the northern part of the county.

At the present time, about 75 percent of the land in Berkshire is in forest—nearly all of it second growth. Compare this to a hundred years ago when 75 percent of the land was open. The only remaining traces of the primeval forest border bogs and gorges where neither livestock nor lumbermen found things to their liking.

Somewhere across Berkshire County is the northern edge of the border between the more southern oak-hickory group of trees and the northern hardwoods. It would be convenient if the trees recognized boundaries that could be drawn on a map. But varying climatic conditions and different elevations make it impossible for a few of the hardier oaks and related trees to know that they are far from their home base. In like fashion, there are sprinkled across Berkshire trees that one would normally expect to find at more northerly latitudes. In north county, there are more beeches, sugar maples, yellow and paper birches, and hemlocks than one finds in the southern part of the county. At especially high elevations there are even red spruce and balsam fir, both generally associated with points well north of the Berkshires. An explanation lies in the theory of botanists that every foot up in elevation is equivalent to about two-thirds of a mile north. Compared to the floor of the Hoosac River Valley at Adams, for instance, which is 750 feet above sea level, the habitat at the summit of nearby Mt. Greylock, which is 2700 feet higher, should be in keeping with that of northern Quebec. This may seem rather far-fetched, but the point to remember is that trees such as elms, chestnuts, and willows, all of which thrive at lower elevations, could not make it at the top of Mt. Greylock. It takes no more than a short drive on a cool fall evening out of one of the valleys and up into the Taconic or the Hoosac range to discover that temperatures vary dramatically according to elevation.

Other determinants in both plant and wildlife habitats are drainage, amount of sunlight, and population density. On the south side of a mountain you might well see a completely different group of trees than on the north. And whereas bolder types such as raccoons and seagulls frequent city yards and town dumps, shy creatures such as the black bear and the common raven are only going to be found where there is plenty of space to roam undisturbed.

The entire county was, before the arrival of the white man, heavily forested. Probably the only open areas in the dense covering were meadows along riverbanks and exposed, rocky ledges where no plant could get a foothold. At first settlers only cleared enough space for their own cultivation and pasturage, but later there was such a demand for timber that logging was done for profit. The supply seemed endless, and little care was taken to conserve this impressive natural resource — the primeval forest. Profits were made, but wood was so plentiful that, when earlier settlers decided they had had enough of the harsh existence in the county and decided to move on, they burned down their houses and from the ashes collected the nails for their next building project.

While the stands of assorted hardwoods stretched 100 feet into the air, they were dominated by the lordly white pine which sometimes reached heights of 150 feet. It was these pines that first felt the logger's ax. There was an early and persistent demand for pine from the English, who used it for building ships, and fights with the colonists over rights to the pines were common. The pine tree became a hot political issue; colonial troops designed a flag with a pine tree on it which flew over Bunker Hill during the famous battle there. Massachusetts later adopted a naval ensign with a pine tree as part of the motif.

To satisfy the demand, the white pine was harvested

almost to extinction. When it was gone, mixed hardwood stands began to develop, chief among them the American chestnut. But this, too, eventually disappeared as it was clear cut in the early 1800s for use in the iron industry. Chestnuts were burned to make charcoal which was used in the great iron furnaces. The wood from the tree was also used to make furniture, fencing, and musical instruments. The bark had a high content of tannin which made it suitable for use in tanneries, and the nutritious nuts were harvested as well. Around 1900 a fungus disease from eastern Asia hit the American chestnut and sickened it rapidly. In one generation, this dominant forest species was destroyed, and today only a few old stumps survive. From these stumps, new trees occasionally sprout, but they rarely get more than six or eight inches in diameter. Recently, larger trees have been found and some have even had fruits, but all eventually succumb to the blight.

Some of these struggling chestnuts can be found on the lower slopes of Mt. Everett, along with birches, maples, and oaks. Pines and scrub oaks predominate near the top where blueberry enthusiasts have found delightful and productive picking in season. Within easy walking distance of the top of Mt. Everett is Guilder Pond which, along with Berry Pond in the Pittsfield State Forest, is one of the highest flat bodies of water in the state. To the south of the summit is Plantain Pond around which bog-type plants such as leatherleaf, sundew, cranberry, and pitcher-plant thrive. Water from the pond plunges over Bear Rock Falls and finds its way to Schenob Brook Swamp in the valley below. There is good birding in the swamp where it is possible to find rails and, with exceptional luck, a chat or two. The summit of Mt. Everett—known as "the Dome" because of its full, rounded profile—is the best place to find an overview of south county. The Dome crowns the Mt. Washington plateau area of the Taconics. To the north, Mt. Greylock is visible on a clear day as are the Catskills and Shawangunks across the Hudson River Valley to the west. Looking south several other Taconic peaks dwindle down into Connecticut. To the east is the Housatonic Valley, sprinkled with small towns and farms; beyond it the Berkshire Barrier, from a distance, does not look as imposing as its name implies.

Not far from Everett, there are a number of fascinating small limestone knolls. From the distance, they rise as small stone haystacks draped with vegetation. The most famous and most often visited is Bartholomew's Cobble in Ashley Falls. The knoll perches on the edge of one of the many meanders that occur throughout the broad flat valley of the Housatonic.

The Cobble can't be put down. For many years a local picnic site, it is now a haven for botanists and naturalists. The hours can drift by in this world of lilliputian ferns, spacious pines, seasoned hemlocks, and weathered rocks of gnarled shapes and postures. Habitats and conditions are quite varied. From the deep darkness of an evergreen grove with drizzling, wet rocks, a trail will lead into dazzling sunlight and a meadow with huge boulders emerging at strange angles from the soil. The Cobble is a quiet place, full of spirits; visitors whisper and their footsteps can hardly be heard.

There is a strong force working here, and many people come back again and again to experience it. Maybe it is the age that counts, that makes people shift gears here. The marble and quartzite that make up the north and south knolls may be some of the oldest rock in the world. Both kinds of rocks were formed between 400 million and 500 million years ago. They were initially laid down as sediments under an inland sea that once covered the southern Berkshires. Both were then rock-hardened as internal heat and pressures twisted and folded and squeezed the material, making it flow like molten plastic. The rock then cooled, slowly, to its present condition. The marble was once limestone, a sedimentary rock formed underneath the sea and made up of shellfish and other calcium-bearing animals that died and sank to the bottom to be recycled; 500 million years later it cropped up in Berkshire County, over 125 miles from the present Atlantic Ocean. Likewise, the quartzite, once living as layers of sand in the shallows of the ocean, has been transformed into a new life atop a small hill 675 feet above Boston and New York.

The rocks at Bartholomew's are not dead; their shapes continually change, although the changes are not noticeable from year to year. But over time, rain, snow, wind, and plants play out their role in the natural scheme of things, and slowly break down the quartzite and marble, grain by grain, piece by piece, section by section. Bartholomew's Cobble will be, sometime, all back in the sea again.

The Cobble has an overwhelming sense of nature undisturbed. It is not brash wilderness, certainly, but more like a fine garden, naturally growing and naturally selecting. The trees are hearty and are represented by oaks, hickories, birches, maples, pines, hemlocks, and red cedars. Many of the elms have been destroyed by the Dutch Elm disease which struck in the 1920s.

If you stopped a visitor and asked why he came, he might say, "the ferns, of course." The sweet soil produced by the marble and the acid soil of the woodland have produced a vast array of lush ferns, many rare and some unique. The Trustees of Reservations, who own and manage the property, list over forty ferns and fern allies. Many of these ferns are labeled, but most are not so that samplers will not wipe out the supply.

Some ferns grow directly on the rocks, living precariously in minute crevices. Visitors travel hundreds of miles to see the walking fern, wall rue, maidenhair spleenwort, ebony spleenwort, and purple stemmed cliffbrake clinging to the rock outcroppings. These are delicate but tenacious ferns of rare fine beauty. Protected and cared for at Bartholomew's Cobble, they will always serve as a reminder of the need to maintain places where plants and animals can live undisturbed by both overzealous naturalists and callous land dealers.

Wildflower buffs will not be disappointed at the Cobble; it is a good place to observe the seasonal procession of flowers. Early flowers like hepatica, bloodrot, rue anemone and early saxifrage are soon followed by the soft bloom of the apple trees. The season continues with columbine, flowing down the rocks, and the great lobelia, with its feet near the Housatonic River. In quiet corners of the woodland, the bishop's cap rise up and fall away, most often unseen. Under the evergreens, the flowering wintergreen shows pink flowers, but only for a short period of time. The hawkweed and the white daisy become field companions in the summer, each flourishing in time to share those long quiet days when the sky is cloudless and the only sound comes from the honey bees making the same rounds they have been making for thousands of years. Late summer brings astors and goldenrods; at the Cobble, twenty-five species of these related plants have been found.

A fifteen-acre ridge in Lenox serves one of the most interesting ecological functions in the Berkshires. A 1975 gift to Massachusetts Audubon's Pleasant Valley Sanctuary, this parcel is the only land in the eastern United States designated solely for the protection of salamanders. The story is an interesting one. Around 1970, field researcher James D. Lazell, then a graduate student at Harvard University, began to notice a decline in the population of spotted salamanders in eastern Massachusetts. On night excursions he observed that the number of salamanders coming to ponds to breed was decreasing dramatically.

The answer to the population decline was found in research being done on acid rains in eastern forests. Acid rains result from the burning of fossil fuels—oil, gas, and coal. Sulfur oxides released during the burning of these fuels are changed into sulfuric acid in the atmosphere. This acid becomes part of the rainwater that eventually finds its way into streams and ponds. The high acid content of water falling on eastern forests was killing the embryos of spotted and Jefferson salamanders. The picture was grim, but a light suddenly emerged in the southern Berkshires. At the Pleasant Valley Sanctuary, salamanders were coming into the ponds in late March and early April as usual. Eggs were being laid, embryos were developing, and the general cycle of things was going on as it had for hundreds of years.

Why were the salamanders able to carry out their full cycle in the Berkshires, yet suffer such great losses in other areas? The answer to the success of these amphibians was found on the high ridge adjacent to the sanctuary lands. The rocks that underlay the ridge were rich in limestone. Limestone is considered a sweetener to soil and water; it neutralizes acidic conditions. Sweet water from the ridge was finding its way down the watershed into the sanctuary ponds and neutralizing the acid in them, creating fine breeding conditions for the native salamanders.

The fifteen-acre ridge was acquired and is now one of the most fascinating and valuable pieces of land in the state, as salamander research continues there. The behavior of the salamanders is watched closely in hopes of finding answers about acid rains and other pollutants in the environment.

Both the red and grey fox can be seen throughout the county. From a distance, it is possible to mistake a fox for a small dog. But a trained eye can tell the shape, movement, and wildness characteristic of the animal. The red fox is bright yellowish red on the sides and somewhat brown on the top. The nose is black as are the backs of the feet and legs.

The red fox weaves an interesting thread through the mixed hardwoods, pastures, and bumpy farmlands of the area. Wild and cautious as he may be, he is also curious. With some regularity, red foxes have been seen trotting among grazing cattle and sheep, and there are records of them entering dooryards and playing with dogs. Farmers who worry about the fox in the chicken coop should be more concerned about the skunk and raccoon. The fox is generally too busy pursuing mice and other small mammals to be bothered with chickens, although an occasional one may be taken when times are bad. Fox roam around five miles from their dens; they are never very far from seclusion and protection since they can travel up to twenty-eight miles per hour. Dens are usually in the woods and are often used for many generations. The den is not well camouflaged, but the tunnels are deep and often elaborate. This home is used during the denning or gestation season which occurs in late winter and early spring. After that, it gets little use except as a hideout. Otherwise, this mammal sleeps in the snow or among the rocks and leaves.

Populations of red fox rise and fall with a predictable rhythm primarily related to the increase and decline of the disease called mange. Other diseases that limit the lifespan of these animals are distemper, heartworm, tularemia, and rickets. A sick, starving fox is a sad looking animal. During low cycles, it may hang around towns and farms looking for easy handouts. During good years, there is nothing as beautiful as a red fox, coat glistening and full, as it trots gracefully across the top of newly fallen and powdery snow.

The grey fox is also a common inhabitant of the area. Preferring the deep woodlands, it is more secretive than the red fox. While the red fox may be seen almost anytime of the night or day, the grey is mostly nocturnal, seeking its food after the sun goes down.

Black bear sightings are less common in the southern Berkshires than in the north. While bears have been seen in the area of Mt. Frissel and along the ridges above Great Barrington, they are more common in the higher and more sparsely populated areas of the Hoosacs and Taconics. Their population has fluctuated over the past hundred years according to habitat changes and hunting practices. Like a number of other southern New England mammals, bears are basically night foragers. Usually hunting alone, they can cover considerable distances—up to fifteen miles from home and sometimes more. Research has shown that the black bear's territory covers a range of nearly eighty square miles.

Mature bears can attain a length of six feet and weigh as much as 600 pounds. They have been clocked at over thirty miles per hour in short bursts through the forest. For the most part they are harmless, although you should take care not to wander between a sow and her cubs or too near a food cache. Prior to 1970, there was a ten-week hunting season for bear in the state. Pressure from conservationists, however, persuaded the Massachusetts Division of Fisheries and Game to limit the season to six days. This new limit has enhanced the rate of survival, but it would seem logical for the black bear to be protected from hunters altogether, since it is currently estimated that there are not more than 100 bears in the state.

For some, the idea of seeing a bear while hiking or driving through the countryside would be a delightful experience. To others it would be terrifying. The adventurous who actually set out to find such an animal will not find it easy—the population is low and the animals are shy. However, there are likely areas to find bear. In general, they like to hunt and play near running water. In the fall, they may be found near oak forests, feeding quietly on acorns.

There are well-trodden bear trails along which are

52

Natural History

"marked trees" that have been clawed and bitten. This practice may be associated with territorialism; no one knows for sure. But if you find a trail with fresh markings, you can be sure an animal is in the vicinity.

Close encounters with bears can be frightening. A bear may rear up imposingly on its hind legs. This is an awesome and threatening maneuver, but remember that it also gives the animal a chance to look over its shoulder to see the best escape route. This is not to suggest that a wild bear is not dangerous. They can attack, but, like most wild animals, they are not interested in confrontation and would rather go about their business of finding food, raising their young, and sleeping.

White-tailed deer are fond of the thousands of rolling acres of high, dry woodland on the Berkshire Barrier, from the Sandisfield State Forest north through the Peru State Forest. Deer also thrive in the territory of October Mountain and across the Housatonic Valley in the forests of the Taconics. They like mixed terrain and enjoy old apple orchards and second growth pastures, where they can browse the tender shoots of berry bushes, red cedars, grey birch, and sweet fern.

Eastern coyotes are moving into Massachusetts from the Adirondacks. These are not the so-called "coydogs" that have received so much interest lately among scientists and hunters, but are true coyotes. These dog-like scavengers are elusive, preferring to get their food by night, but they can be seen at any time of the day or night.

Bobcat sightings continue, particularly in the Taconics, but the population is apparently not large. Bobcats tend to be nocturnal and solitary, although they sometimes make their presence known by a blood-curdling cry that can wake you with a jolt. Smaller mammals that are common in low-lying areas include the skunk, raccoon, mink, opossum, woodchuck, beaver, muskrat, and cottontail rabbit. The snowshoe hare prefers the uplands. Sometimes called the varying hare, it has the ability to change its camouflage from brown in summer to nearly pure white in winter. In remote, higher regions such as the Savoy Mountain State Forest, mammals such as the fisher-cat, pine marten, and eastern cougar are spotted now and then by those who know what to look for.

Tales about rattlesnakes on the Mt. Washington plateau are told around warm fireplaces at night and shared by farmers with neighbors across the fence during the day. Many of the stories are true. There have been successful scientific expeditions into this sparsely populated and semi-wilderness area. As a result, however, the rattlesnake population has been severely diminished. Fewer and fewer herpetologists make the trip to the area as active dens become more and more difficult to find. Still, rattlesnakes can be considered more common and are occasionally seen by hikers, motorists, and bicyclists. In addition to the Mt. Washington plateau, there are isolated pockets on East Mountain near Great Barrington and on Lenox Mountain.

The timber rattler is the common rattlesnake of the Northeast. Usually it has black or dark brown crossbands on a field of yellow to dark brown or black, but some are solid black. These snakes feed on frogs, mice, and birds. The latin name *Crotalus horridus horridus* is enough to raise hairs on the neck. The snake is large (up to five feet long) and impressive, but bites are extremely rare and almost never fatal. These reptiles should be treated with respect and given plenty of time to leave a trail if they are encountered taking in the sun. The rattler plays a part in the great web of nature and should not be killed or attacked.

Other snakes of interest in the Berkshires are the red-bellied snake, water snake, garter snake, ribbon snake, ring-neck snake, green snake, and copperhead.

Natural History

Bird life varies according to habitat. At higher elevations population density dwindles, although there are some species that will only frequent the highlands. Colorful migrant warblers prefer the higher areas, particularly where there are streams and ponds. Examples are the Blackburnian warbler, Louisiana waterthrush, Cape May warbler, and black-throated blue warbler. Some dozen species of warblers have been reported nesting on Mt. Greylock. The red-tailed hawk, the broad-winged hawk, and the goshawk all prefer the higher elevations for nesting, especially in areas that are heavily wooded. Listen for the high-pitched whistle of these predators as they hunt over high country ravines and hills.

On shallow bodies of water, an occasional great blue heron may wade into view or startle you as it flies by with an impressive six-foot wing span. You might catch sight of a black-crowned night heron or possibly a little green heron. Look for the herons at places like Mill Pond in Egremont or Cheshire Reservoir. These and other similar bodies of water will attract ducks such as the redhead, ring-necked, golden-eye, and old-squaw. During the fall migration, these ducks are apt to be joined by Canada and snow geese, whistling swans, and even herring and Bonaparte's gulls. The highly decorated wood duck is not uncommon on bodies of water such as Plantain Pond in Mt. Washington, South Pond in Savoy, or Windsor Pond in Windsor. Mallards and black ducks are the most common dabblers. Look out onto a pond with a pair of field glasses and mallards will quite regularly be the first ducks in sight.

The Housatonic River supports a modest population of ducks, especially where it widens into lagoons. Particularly good viewing can be done between Canoe Meadows, a sanctuary of the Massachusetts Audubon Society in Pittsfield, and Woods Pond Dam downriver. This twelve-mile strip contains about 1400 acres, and much of it is in the public domain. Reasonable care should be taken in these areas during hunting season.

The familiar rattle of the kingfisher can be heard along the larger streams and ponds—even into the winter months if there is still some open water. They put on quite a show as they hover over the water waiting for a fish to come near enough to the surface for a kill. If, after a successful plunge, they find the fish too large to swallow in one gulp, they will fly to a branch or rock and beat the prey against the hard object until it is tenderized.

In September and October, you might want to search out an advantageous site from which to observe the fall migration of hawks. Spruce Hill in the Savoy Mountain State Forest and Monument Mountain in Great Barrington come to mind, but there are many other suitable spots. Broad-winged and red-tailed hawks will pass by throughout the day in a spectacular display of soaring and circling on the thermal currents fueled by heat from the valley below and southerly breezes. Lucky viewers may catch a glimpse of a bald eagle. Turkey vultures glide by seemingly within arm's reach, with their featherless heads cocked so that they can get a view of the spectators below. At ground level, towhees, often in large numbers, scratch in the leaves for tidbits.

Winter brings waves of snow buntings, reeling like schools of fish in the air. Redpolls, pine siskins, and grosbeaks work to survive in the harsh weather. Red and white crossbills move in flocks from one feeding site to the next. The rough-legged hawk, a rare visitor from the north country, may be seen hunting over snow-covered fields. Another winter visitor, usually seen by itself perched at the very top of a tree, is the northern shrike, or butcherbird. This predator has a habit of impaling its prey, such as meadow moles, on hawthorn spikes. The butcherbird can be confused with a mockingbird; telltale differences are an especially dark mask around the eyes and its predatory behavior.

Natural History

Ruffed grouse are also prevalent during the winter months when one of their favorite spots is a stand of hemlocks. Though winter is the low ebb for bird life, there are some sixty species present in the Berkshires. You cannot miss the chickadee whose distinctive call will remind you that you are a threatening intruder in the woods. If you stay still and offer a few sunflower seeds in your hand, you may find that the chickadee is not so threatened after all. White- and red-breasted nuthatches, often seen hitching up and down tree trunks, have a call that is as friendly as any of the winter songs.

Squawking blue jays do not seem to disturb the brown creepers that are busy digging out grubs from underneath the bark of tree trunks. Hairy and downy woodpeckers bang away with their pointed bills on dead limbs, hoping to find a daily supplement. Juncos, flicking their white-lined tails like deer on the run, feed on the open ground. And tree sparrows work over the weed patches and the alder and birch catkins.

With the return of the warm months, bird life increases dramatically. One cannot help but feel that spring is on the way when an Eastern bluebird is spotted showing off its iridescent blue coloring. Bluebirds were once fairly common breeders in the Berkshires, but due to the introduction of the starling and the house sparrow, the bluebird rarely breeds here nowadays. The starling evicts the bluebird from its nesting sites and the house sparrow breaks the eggs of the bluebird. Bobolinks and meadowlarks both like to nest along the edges of fields, but both are being driven out by land development and agricultural interferences.

Swarms of insects, while a nuisance to man, delight the returning birds. It is a treat to watch a great crested flycatcher swoop through a cloud of insects for a meal, then return to its perch. Swallows and sparrows may weight down a telephone wire as they rest for a moment before moving on. Near them, you might catch sight of a kingbird; but do not stray too near if it is nesting, since the kingbird, giving credence to its name, will attack any intruder, no matter how large or small.

Orioles and vireos nest in tree-shaded villages. The graceful elms were once alive with nests, but the trees have been attacked by the European elm beetle and the Dutch elm disease that follows. Phoebes and wrens seem to enjoy nesting sites near people as well. A shyer creature is the screech owl who will only be about when it is dark. He may be perched on a fence post waiting for the movement of a small rodent or bird.

Southern birds like the tufted titmouse, the cardinal, and the mockingbird have been stretching their territorial limits further north and are becoming residents of the Berkshires. The northern influence is seen with the siskins, redpolls, grosbeaks, and crossbills—beautiful birds which lend color and activity to the otherwise starved winter months.

From the Dome in the south to Greylock's dominance in the north, the mountains, waterways, fields, upland pastures, lakes, ponds, and swamps of Berkshire County lend themselves to natural history study and investigation. Happily, there is plenty of public land open for just that purpose, and an almost endless network of trails weaves its way through the county, providing access to those who let their curiosity and their feet take them where they may.

(All of the research and most of the writing for this chapter was done by Dan Hart and Charles Quinlan.)

Walking Trails

Berkshire County is loaded with opportunities for anyone who wants to walk away from it all. While there is no real wilderness left in the county, a little effort will leave you with the impression that you are much farther from civilization than is actually the case. In Savoy Mountain State Forest, for example, you can wander through some of the most wild terrain in the state, within a few miles — as the crow flies — of the center of North Adams. In the opposite corner of the county, the rugged isolation of Mt. Washington State Forest belies the fact that the area is less than 100 miles from Manhattan.

Although there is no spot in the county that is more than five miles from a paved (or, in winter, plowed) road, care should be taken in the woods, especially if you are traveling alone. Trouble can be avoided if you pay attention to the suggestions that follow and stir in some common sense for good measure. While many of tips may seem obvious, it cannot hurt to have them spelled out.

First of all, it is a good idea to know what kind of condition you are in. If you have not walked a distance of five miles in the last few years, you should not assume you can do it now without at least some discomfort. Take a short walk over easy terrain for starters — sort of a shake-down cruise. You might find that everything is running smoothly and that you are ready to tackle anything that this book or the Berkshires have to offer. On the other hand, you may discover that boots that fit a few years back now cause blistering, or that legs that carried you up and over the White Mountains or the Rockies do not have the snap they once had. If you find a flaw, the time to find a remedy is before you head out on a longer, more strenuous walk, not after the fact when you may be aching so badly that you will swear off walking forever.

The time estimates provided with each trail description are based, for the most part, on steady walking. When moving briskly over a level trail, you should be able to cover a mile in fifteen to twenty minutes. When you run into more hilly terrain, your pace will obviously slacken. Plan your walk early enough in the day so that you will not be forced to scurry down a mountainside in the dark. It is also a good idea to have a notion of what the weather is going to do. Unless you are prepared for a drenching, stay off the trails when heavy rain is forecast. In the middle of the summer, one can survive a downpour with only a bit of discomfort. A similar shower in early May or late October might be driven by high winds and include some sleet, a combination which could test your tolerance for exposure.

Though it is a nuisance to overburden yourself with equipment that turns out to be unnecessary, you will be happy to have it should you find yourself in a threatening situation. Of course you would not be going into the woods in the first place if you did not enjoy a little adventure and were not willing to take a few chances. The point is that it is foolish to load the deck against yourself. People have found themselves in serious predicaments in the more remote sections of the Berkshire, usually because they did not know what they were getting in for and did not take a few minutes before they set out to think about where they were going and how to get there and back.

Walking Trails

Let someone know where you are going and when you expect to return. There are registers at several of the trailheads and most of the state forests are manned every day of the year. I have never been lost for more than a few minutes and I have never been injured walking the Berkshires, but I have walked alone many times. In some instances, I did not let anyone know where I was, a foolish oversight which I have decided not to repeat. Had I ever run into any trouble, I could have spent many anxious hours (especially in the off-season) waiting alone in the woods, hoping that someone would happen upon me or notice that my car had been in the parking area for an exceptionally long time.

Never go into unfamiliar woods without a compass, a map, and a clear impression of the location of the nearest road. If you do not know how to use a compass or read a map, take the time to find out from someone who does. Study the map to determine the road nearest to the trail so that you can follow the shortest route out of the woods should it become necessary. In order to follow the trails described in this book, a watch is also needed, since many of the distances are measured in minutes, not miles.

Other equipment you should carry in a small pack includes a canteen, snack (cheese, nuts, chocolate, raisins, and the like are best for quick energy), first-aid kit, snakebite kit (the likelihood of tangling with a rattler is almost nil, but who needs to take chances?), insect repellant, flashlight, whistle (three blasts if you need help), pocket knife, matches, extra socks, sweater, and poncho or rain parka. For overnight trips, you will also need a tent, sleeping bag, food, and eating and cooking utensils — including a stove. Camping in the state forest is confined to the campgrounds listed on page 64-65. Fires are not permitted outside of the campgrounds.

Most of the walks described in this book are short enough so that special footgear is not necessary. In other words, you will not run into "Disaster on the Trail" if you are caught walking in a pair of sturdy shoes or even sneakers. By wearing such mundane shoes, you will save a bundle and may end up suffering nothing worse than the scorn of equipment freaks who stomp by with their feet encased in expensive, *imported* boots and with their noses in the air. On the other hand there is much to be said for a good pair of properly fitted boots with lug soles. Once you break them in and get used to the feel of walking in them, you may find yourself wondering how you ever got by with those flimsy sneakers that left you with sore ankles and blistered feet after a day on the trail. Once you find a comfortable stride, the boots seem to develop a momentum of their own; you can just lie back and let the boots do the walking.

If you start out on a walk in the early morning when the temperature is still cool, long pants may be appropriate. As the day warms, however, and your body with it, the pant legs may start sticking to your thighs, making every step seem more arduous. Consider carrying a pair of shorts in your pack. It is not a bad idea to carry enough extra clothing so that you can either add or subtract one layer, depending on the temperature and precipitation. In winter, of course, you will have to add layers at the outset. There is no substitute for an insulated parka with a hood to go over everything else you may have on. Waterproof boots have their place as well; with them you can slosh through almost anything. If there is snow on the ground, a pair of gaiters, or leggings, will keep the snow out of your boots. Wet feet can sap the body of heat and energy before you can conjure up an image of sitting in front of a nice warm fire. When planning a walk in the winter woods, it is wise to be more conservative than you might be at other times of the year, since the elements are obviously less forgiving and there are fewer people on the trails if you happen to run into trouble.

To supplement the maps that accompany each trail

description in this book, you might want to carry U.S. Geological Survey topographical maps. These maps (sold by local outdoor equipment stores and by U.S. Geological Survey, Reston, VA 22092) may be particularly helpful in providing an overview of specific areas. They do not, however, show all the footpaths described in the walks that follow this chapter. The headquarters of individual state forests provide maps free of charge, but most of them were drawn in the 1930s by the Civilian Conservation Corps and they are obviously outdated. Some of them have been updated in the last few years, but as a whole they are not very reliable.

The system for marking trails in the state forests is almost as undependable as the maps. The general rule is that blue triangular markers denote foot trails, orange triangles mark snowmobile trails, and red triangles signify bridle paths. These markers rarely stay attached to the trees, however, as competing interests see it their duty to remove as many of the blazes as possible. There is no love lost between hikers and four-wheel drive addicts, for example, and each group blames the other for removing many of the blazes. One wonders why the state forest planners do not use painted blazes instead of the wooden triangles which are so easy to tear down. It is a shame that the trails are so poorly marked in the state forests. In comparison, trail planners at Notchview Reservation, Monument Mountain Reservation, and Pleasant Valley Wildlife Sanctuary have done a fine job of laying out trails as well as marking and maintaining them.

When you venture out onto some of the trails described in this book, then, be prepared for a scarcity of blazes. In a way this is not such a bad turn of events, since it forces you to use your head and think about where you are heading. When trails are over-marked, it is easy to fall into a lethargic state—you simply follow along from one blaze to the next without having to think at all.

The trails described in this book can be similarly

unstimulating if you only and always choose to follow them to the letter of the law. Do not hesitate to use them as general references from which you can deviate as much as you like, incorporating ideas of your own after studying the topographical maps. You might choose to combine one of the walks with a nearby stretch of trail or back road that you have heard about from a friend or discovered on the maps. For example, in a number of places you can hook up with the Appalachian Trail (see Greylock Loop and Mt. Wilcox), which runs the entire length of the county, and turn a day hike into an almost limitless trek. The following trails, written up as ski trails, also make fine walking trails: Ashley Hill Brook Trail (which can connect with the Alander Mountain trail via the South Taconic Trail), Bartholomew's Cobble, Abbey Hill, and North Pond.

There are public campgrounds in several of the state forests which you might choose to use should you decide to expand one or more of these walks, or if you are simply looking for a place to stay overnight. A list of the campgrounds follows:

BEARTOWN STATE FOREST: 12 campsites; water; outhouses; $3.00 per night; first come, first served; phone 413-528-0904.

CLARKSBURG STATE PARK (Mauserts Pond Area): 47 campsites; water; outhouses; $4.00 per night; first come, first served; phone 413-664-9030.

SAVOY MOUNTAIN STATE FOREST: 45 campsites; flush toilets; showers; $4.00 per night; first come, first served; phone 413-663-8469. In addition, there are 3 cabins which can be reserved at $8.00 per night.

WINDSOR STATE FOREST: 24 campsites; water; outhouses; $3.00 per night; first come, first served; phone 413-684-9760.

MONROE STATE FOREST: 3 Vermont shelters; no water; outhouses; no phone. Contact Visitor Center at Bear Swamp Pumped Power Project on River Road.

Walking Trails

MT. GREYLOCK STATE RESERVATION: 35 campsites; water; outhouses; $3.00 per night; first come, first served; phone 413-499-4262.

PITTSFIELD STATE FOREST: 31 campsites; water; $4.00 per night with flush toilets; $3.00 per night with outhouses; first come, first served; phone 413-442-8992.

OCTOBER MOUNTAIN STATE FOREST: 50 campsites; water; $4.00 per night with flush toilets; $3.00 per night with outhouses; first come, first served; phone 413-243-9735.

SANDISFIELD STATE FOREST (West Lake Area): 5 backpack sites; no water; no outhouses; $1.00 per night; first come, first served; phone 413-258-4774.

TOLLAND STATE FOREST: 90 campsites; water; flush toilets; $4.00 per night; first come, first served; phone 413-269-7268.

MT. WASHINGTON STATE FOREST: 10 backpack sites; no water; pit toilet; $1.00 per night; first come, first served; phone 413-528-0330.

WALKER'S CHECKLIST:

Wristwatch	Flashlight
Compass	Whistle
Map	Pocketknife
Canteen	Extra socks
Snack	Sweater
First-aid kit	Shorts
Snakebite kit	Poncho or rain parka
Insect repellant	

And leave the trails cleaner than you found them.

Alander Mountain

Territory: Mt. Washington State Forest
Trail Length: 7 miles.
Start: Parking area at Mt. Washington State Forest Headquarters.
Finish: Same.
Highest Point: Alander Mountain (2239 feet).
Vertical Rise: 790 feet
Time Estimate: 3½ hours
USGS Quadrangle: Bashbish Falls.

Directions to trailhead: From Great Barrington, follow Rte. 23 west towards South Egremont and Hillsdale, New York. Just past the center of S. Egremont, turn left (south) on Rte. 41. Within a few hundred yards and just after a swampy pond on the right, turn right onto Mt. Washington Rd. Follow this road along a straight stretch for about 2 mi. when suddenly the road plunges into the Taconic Range. Once the road gets into the town of Mt. Washington, there are 2 roads that join it from the right (west); bear left at each intersection. Eight mi. after the intersection between Mt. Washington Rd. and Rte. 41, the road passes the entrance to Mt. Everett Reservation on the left. Stay on what is now called East St. and go straight ahead at the intersection ¼ mi. past the entrance to the reservation. Another mile will bring you to the State Forest Headquarters on the right. The parking area is behind the garage that houses the headquarters.

Trail description: From the parking lot, follow the blue triangular markers that are used in this and other state forests to denote foot trails. The trail heads west and crosses a field before entering the woods after a few hundred yards. It soon emerges from the woods and descends gradually through another field. At the bottom of this field, the trail

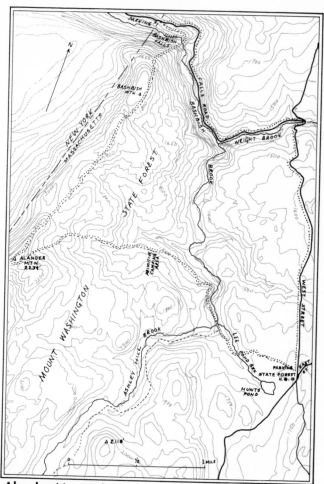

Alander Mountain

angles to the left and then to the right past a private dwelling and over Lee Pond Brook via a wooden bridge. From the bridge the trail follows an old woods road until, after 5 minutes, it divides. To the left at this intersection is the Ashley Hill Brook Trail. To the right is the Alander Mtn. Trail.

Turn right onto the Alander Mtn. Trail which, after a couple of minutes, crosses Ashley Hill Brook. As of late 1978 there was no bridge across the brook, but it is easy enough to ford. Once across the brook, the trail beings to climb steadily but gently along an old woods road. A mile up this trail you will pass a so-called "Primitive Camping Area" on the left. The blue markers stop at this point, but it is not difficult to find your way from here.

Ten minutes after leaving the turnoff for the campground, there is a fork in the trail. Bear left and continue to climb. After another 10 minutes the road, which is now paralleling a small brook, comes to a tight, circular clearing. Just after this clearing the woods road terminates and the trail becomes a narrow footpath, often working its way through clumps of laurel. The path continues to parallel the brook which gradually diminishes to a trickle. About a mile after the clearing, the trail comes to a small cabin which nestles in the notch between the twin peaks of Alander Mtn. The cabin is owned and maintained by the state forest. Walk about 20 yds. past the cabin and look for red paint blazes on the right. Follow these blazes to the open western summit of Alander Mtn. and be prepared for one of the most breath-taking views in all of Berkshire County.

To the west lies the Harlem Valley in New York State with the Catskill Mountains in the background. When the air is dry and the visibility unlimited, you can make out the taller buildings in Albany, almost 50 mi. to the northwest. To the south and east, Brace Mtn. in New York and Mts. Frissell, Ashley, Race, and Everett define the shape of the South Taconic Highland. Mt. Everett dominates the eastern

Walking Trails

horizon as it towers above the town of Mt. Washington in the foreground. Nearly one-half of the total acreage in the town of Mt. Washington is public land. While this may seem like an extreme proportion, consider that it is equaled or exceeded in the other Berkshire towns of Savoy, Washington, and New Ashford.

The summit of Alander is a fine spot for a picnic if the temperature is not too brisk. There are countless spots with wonderful views, so you will not have trouble finding privacy if there are others up there with you. After taking in the sights, you can either retrace your steps to the parking lot (about 1½ hours away), or you can venture off to the north via the South Taconic Trail for a visit to Bashbish Falls the hard way.

If you have the time and the interest to go north, look for white paint blazes on rocks on the north side of the summit. This trail is maintained by the New York-New Jersey Chapter of the Appalachian Trail Conference even though it is within the boundaries of Mt. Washington State Forest. The trail wanders along the high ridge between Alander and Bashbish Mountains and often emerges from the woods to offer splendid views, although none compare with the panorama from Alander. After 2 mi. the trail comes to the top of Bashbish Mtn. and begins to descend through hemlocks. At times the descent is steep; this trail should not be tackled in winter when there is snow on the ground—it is too slippery. Eventually the trail comes to the edge of a nearly vertical rock face overlooking Bashbish Falls. Sturdy cable fences have been constructed above particulary hazardous spots around the gorge, since there have been a number of accidents involving people who wanted to get just a little closer to the edge.

Follow the trail along the fence to the right (east) and then down a brief but precipitous stretch to the edge of the brook. The stream is not all that big, but the depth of the gorge gives testimony to the tenacity of the stream, as it has worn away everything but the hardest bedrock and is still working at that. Follow the brook upstream for a few yards where the trail crosses to the other side. You may have to do some wading to get across as makeshift bridges are often washed downstream. Once you are on the north side of the brook, follow the trail up to the parking area on Falls Rd.

If you choose to walk back to the parking lot at the State Forest Headquarters via the easy route, turn right (east) onto Falls Rd. and walk up along the stream until it reaches West St. at the first intersection you come to. The distance between the falls parking area and West St. is about 1¼ mi. Turn right onto West St. and walk 2 mi. back to the State Forest Headquarters.

If, on the other hand, you cannot stand to end the day without another visit to the top of Alander, retrace your steps across the stream and begin the hard climb up Bashbish Mtn. (Another possibility for this walk — if you have two cars at your disposal — is to leave one car at the falls parking area early in the day. Then drive to the State Forest Headquarters and start the walk from there as described above.)

New Marlborough Byways

Territory: South-central New Marlborough just north of the Connecticut border.
Trail Length: 11 miles.
Start: Campbell Falls Picnic Area.
Finish: Same.
Highest Point: 1400 feet.

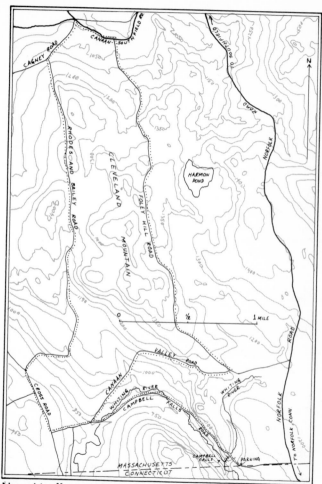

New Marlborough Byways

Vertical Rise: 550 feet.
Time Estimate: 4 hours.
USGS Quadrangles: South Sandisfield and Ashley Falls.

Directions to trailhead: From Great Barrington and the north, follow Rte. 23 east out of Great Barrington for about 5 mi. Turn right onto Rte. 57 and stay on 57 until the village of New Marlborough (about 6 mi.). In New Marlborough, turn right onto New Marlborough-Southfield Rd. Stay on this road for 1½ mi. until the road forks by a bridge on the left. Take the left fork over the bridge onto Norfolk Rd. which immediately passes through the village of Southfield and continues on towards the south. Five mi. after the center of Southfield, Norfolk Rd. crosses the border into Connecticut. Right at the border there is a small road to the right (west) with a sign for Campbell Falls State Park. Take this right and follow the road for just under ½ mi. until it comes to a small picnic area on the left straddling the Massachusetts-Connecticut border. Park here.

From Canaan (Connecticut) and the south, follow Rte. 44 east towards Norfolk. As Rte. 44 enters the village of Norfolk, Rte. 272 turns off to the left and heads north for Massachusetts. Turn left onto Rte. 272 and follow it for about 5 mi. until you see a road off to the left marked "Campbell Falls State Park." Do not take this left but continue on another ¼ mi. until there is another turn to the left with a smaller sign for the falls. This turn is just a few dozen yards past a concrete post marking the state border. Take this second left and follow it just under ½ mi. to the small picnic and parking area for Campbell Falls.

Trail description: This walk follows a connecting link of back roads that are, except for very brief stretches, covered with gravel or dirt. The roads are all open to automobile traffic, but they are not main routes and are used infrequently. Care

Walking Trails

should be taken, of course, to stay out of the way of oncoming cars, but few will be met in the course of the walk. The roads pass by a representative assortment of New England country settings: woodlands, swamps, streams, and open fields; worn homes, sparkling estates, and working farms.

From the picnic area at Campbell Falls turn to the left (northwest) on the road and immediately pass over a fine, stone-faced bridge that takes you over the Whiting River just before it tumbles down Campbell Falls. After the bridge, the road begins a gentle descent until, after a few hundred yards, it is at the same level as the river which now parallels the road on the left. The road crosses the river twice before it intersects with Canaan Valley Rd. 1¼ mi. from the parking lot. On the far (north) side of the intersection, there is a long narrow swamp. Go left onto Canaan Valley Rd., pass over a small creek which drains the swamp, and turn right off of Canaan Valley Rd. within 200 yds. onto another gravel road which climbs up a hill and heads due west. This is the first right off of Canaan Valley Rd. Within 300 yds. this road comes to a triangular intersection with another country lane called Cross Rd. Turn right onto the Cross Rd. and follow it through a forested area until it enters, after ¼ mi., an open area with a weathered farmhouse on the right and a field on the left. Leffingwell Rd. goes off to the left at this point, but you should continue on straight ahead. Take the first turn to the right, ¼ mi. after Leffingwell Rd., onto Rhodes and Bailey Rd.

Rhodes and Bailey Rd. drops down a bit to cross the upper reaches of the same swamp you noticed at the intersection of Canaan Valley and Campbell Falls roads. Then Rhodes and Bailey climbs and twists past a couple of farmhouses and enters the woods. A walk of a mile will take you past an operating, one-family sawmill, a reminder of times past when rural areas like this were sprinkled with small mills of every description. Within another mile, Rhodes and Bailey

73

emerges from the woods and passes between fields such as those that at one time covered nearly 80 percent of the Berkshire countryside.

After 2¾ mi., Rhodes and Bailey Rd. comes to a T with Cagney Rd. next to a white farmhouse and in front of a red barn. Turn right here and follow this extension of Rhodes and Bailey just over ¼ mi. downhill until it comes out onto Canaan-Southfield Rd. Turn hard right here and follow Canaan-Southfield Rd. for about ¼ mi. as it parallels the Umpachene River on the left side of the road. After ¼ mi., Foley Hill Rd., yet another gravel country road, climbs off to the right.

Stay on the main road here for just under 3 mi. After about a mile there is a fork where you should bear right; after about 1¼ mi. there is an overgrown trail leading into the woods on the right. Continue on along the main road. Eventually, 2¾ mi. from Canaan-Southfield Rd., Foley Hill Rd. ends at Canaan Valley Rd. which has power and/or telephone poles running along it. Turn right here onto Canaan Valley Rd. heading southwest from the intersection. This road passes by several homes as it works its way to the west. After about a mile, it passes the Canaan Valley Sporting Club on the right. One-fourth mi. after the Sporting Club, it comes once again to the intersection by the swamp where Campbell Falls Rd. goes off to the left. This is the first intersection you will come to as you walk along Canaan Valley Rd. Turn left onto Campbell Falls Rd. and retrace the first leg of the walk for ¼ mi. back to the picnic area and your car.

Mt. Wilcox

Territory: Beartown State Forest.
Trail Length: 10 miles.
Start: Picnic area at Benedict Pond.
Finish: Same.
Highest Point: Mt. Wilcox (2112 feet).
Vertical Rise: 640 feet.
Time Estimate: 5 hours.
USGS Quadrangles: Great Barrington and Monterey.

Directions to trailhead: From Rte. 7 in Great Barrington, take Rte. 23 to the east for 2½ mi. until there is an intersection where smaller roads go off both to the right and the left. Turn left onto Monument Valley Rd. and follow it until it intersects with Blue Hill Rd. after 1¾ mi. Turn right onto Blue Hill Rd. which is the first paved road to leave Monument Valley Rd. Follow Blue Hill Rd. for just under a mile until it comes to a T intersection. Turn right again here and continue along this extension of Blue Hill Rd. for 1½ mi. until the first left, where there is a sign for Beartown State Forest. Turn left here and follow the hard road for ½ mi. to the picnic and parking area alongside Benedict Pond. During the summer months there is a $2.00 fee for parking here.

Trail description: This walk takes you up and over Mt. Wilcox via the Appalachian Trail, a true interstate of footpaths which runs just over 2,000 mi. from Springer Mtn. in Georgia to Mt. Katahdin in Maine. The trail enters Massachusetts from Connecticut in the town of Mt. Washington and wanders from one mountaintop to the next as it makes its way up through the length of Berkshire County. By the time it passes into Vermont from the town of Clarksburg, it has traveled over 80 mi. in Massachusetts. The trail is marked by white blazes, usually in the form of rec-

Mt. Wilcox

tangles standing on end. Where there are two blazes on one tree, a junction in the trail is signaled.

Because of the increased use of the trail in recent years and because it passes over private property in a number of places, it is constantly being rerouted. The Appalachian Trail Conference (P.O. Box 236, Harpers Ferry, WV 25425) publishes a series of trail guides which describe the entire length of the trail in detail. *Appalachian Trail Guide: Massachusetts-Connecticut* covers the sections of the trail which run through Connecticut and Massachusetts.

As you stand in the parking area at Benedict Pond and look out over the pond, there is a blue-blazed trail to the right of the beach. This section of trail is part of a network of trails maintained by Beartown State Forest. Follow the trail as it heads southeast away from the parking area and along the shore of the pond. The trail continues to hug the shore of the pond for 10 minutes or until it intersects with a road. Turn left onto this road and immediately (5 yds.) pass over a bridge. Within a few yards of the end of the bridge, look for the white rectangular blazes of the Appalachian Trail on the right side of the road. Turn onto the footpath marked by the white rectangles and follow it off to the east. After about 5 minutes the trail begins to climb fairly steeply up a rocky area. At the top it swings off to the south and soon emerges onto a series of ledges from which there is a fine view towards the southwest.

Within 20 minutes the trail intersects with an old woods road marked by telephone poles that runs northwest-southeast. Cross this road and continue to follow the footpath marked by the white blazes. After another 10 minutes of steep climbing over rocky terrain, the trail comes to a hard-surfaced road that services the summit of Mt. Wilcox. The trail crosses this road and continues on towards the north. Stay with the footpath for about another 30 minutes until it comes to the top of Mt. Wilcox, from which, unfortunately, there is no view. There are several towers here, including a fire tower and a couple of radio towers.

From the base of the fire tower, walk a few yards to the northeast and turn right onto the service road. Follow this road for a few hundred yards until it merges with another road. Cut back to the left (north) here and follow this road for 50 yds. At this point the Appalachian Trail turns off to the right and descends into the forest. Follow the white blazes of the trail as it heads in a generally easterly direction. After about 2 mi. or 45 minutes, the trail comes out on Beartown Mtn. Rd. which runs northwest-southeast at this point.

Here you have a choice about the route which will take you back to Benedict Road and the parking lot. You can either retrace your steps over Mt. Wilcox via the same trail you have just walked along, or you can turn right and follow Beartown Mtn. Rd. off to the southeast. If you choose the latter route, you should stay on Beartown Mtn. Rd. for just over 1¼ mi. or until the road makes a 90° swing to the left. At this turn, Brett Rd.—an old town road that is rapidly going to seed—goes off to the right and heads west. Turn right onto Brett and follow it for about 1½ mi. Eventually it passes a couple of red buildings on the right and a clearing on the left. Just past this open space, Brett Rd. drops down a few feet and passes over the beginnings of a brook. Stay on the road for another 300-400 yds. until you notice an overgrown road marked by telephone poles going off to the right (northwest). Turn onto this road and follow it for about a mile, or 20 minutes, when you should keep an eye out on both sides for the white markers of the Appalachian Trail. Turn left at the markers onto the footpath as it descends towards the southwest. Now you are back on the first leg of this walk, and soon you will come upon the ledges from which you looked out over the southwestern part of the county earlier in the day.

From the ledges it is about a 10-minute walk back to the

road which runs along the eastern edge of Benedict Pond.
Turn left onto the road and walk over the bridge. Remember
to look for the blue-blazed trail on the right just after you
cross the bridge. Follow this trail along the edge of the pond
for another 10 minutes until it ends at the parking area.

Monument Mountain

Territory: Monument Mountain Reservation in Great Bar-
    rington.
Trail Length: 2½ miles.
Start: Parking area alongside Route 7.
Finish: Same.
Highest Point: Squaw Peak (1642 feet).
Vertical Rise: 700 feet.
Time Estimate: 2 hours.
USGS Quadrangles: Great Barrington and Stockbridge.

Directions to trailhead: From Stockbridge and the north,
take Rte. 7 going south out of Stockbridge. About 2½ mi. out
of town, you will pass Monument Mountain High School on
the left. Half a mile past the high school there is a large parking area on the right which is marked by signs for Monument
Mountain Reservation.

From Great Barrington and the south, follow Rte. 7 north.
Look for the parking area on the left 1½ mi. after the intersection of Rtes. 7 and 183.

Trail description: The Monument Mountain Reservation is
owned and run by the Trustees of Reservations, the largest
private landholders of conservation areas in the Com-

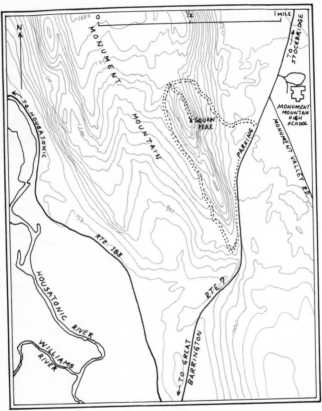

Monument Mountain

monwealth of Massachusetts. The trustees were founded in 1891 by Charles Elliot, a landscape architect who saw the need for the "refreshing power" of open spaces for the population as a whole, which was, at that time, migrating at an ever greater pace from the countryside to the cities. Today, the trustees administer 64 properties across the state.

From the top of Monument Mountain, Indians, according to legend, jumped or were thrown to their deaths on the rocks below when they had offended the gods. On a slightly more sanguine note, Monument Mtn. served as the site of the first meeting between Herman Melville and Nathaniel Hawthorne in August of 1850. With a party of publishers and other writers that included Oliver Wendell Holmes, the two climbed the mountain for a picnic. Though the two had shied away from each other before this encounter, they were to form a tight, if short-lived, friendship after it.

The trail to Squaw Peak starts at the north or right-hand side of the parking lot if you are facing away from the highway. It is marked by white circular blazes. For a few minutes the trail winds along easily over mostly level ground, but then begins a fairly sharp ascent heading generally northwest. The pitch stays steep for about 20 minutes — if you are in shape — until the trail reaches a ridge and divides. Go to the left (south) at this junction and follow the trail as it finds its way to the top of Squaw Peak. Here there is a fascinating jumble of boulders that resembles a breakwater protecting a harbor. You may be tempted to bound from one rock to the next, but take care if you do, as there are some quick drop-offs that are well disguised by underbrush. The view from the top is terrific, although slightly marred by the proximity of Rte. 7. If you can blot out that sight and the noise that goes along with it, you can imagine yourself in a far more remote spot.

Follow the white-blazed trail back down from the summit to the junction mentioned above. On the way down, you should turn to the left here and begin a long, gradual descent that will take you along the west flank of the mountain and eventually around its southern end. Whenever there is an option, stay to the left and follow the white circles. Here, with the mountain blocking Rte. 7, you will find silence and peace. It is something of a shock when the trail comes around the south side of the mountain and dumps you abruptly on the highway. Turn left (north) and walk along the shoulder of the highway about ¼ mi. back to the parking lot.

Kennedy Park

Territory: John D. Kennedy Park in the town of Lenox.
Trail Length: 3½-4 miles.
Start: Kennedy Park parking lot on west side of Main Street (Route 7A).
Finish: Same.
Highest Point: Approximately 1550 feet.
Vertical Rise: 300-400 feet.
Time Estimate: 2 hours.
USGS Quadrangles: Stockbridge and Pittsfield West.

Directions to trailhead: From the center of Lenox, follow Rte. 7A—Main St.—north up the hill past the white Church on the Hill on the left and almost to the interchange with Rtes. 7 and 20. Fifty yds. before an island that separates traffic for the interchange, look for a small parking lot on the left. There is a wooden fence around the outside of the parking lot and a sign which is not easily legible from a car.

From Pittsfield and the north, follow Rte. 7 south until it divides just north of Lenox. Here, take Rte. 7A to the right at the fork and look for the parking lot on the right immediately after the fork.

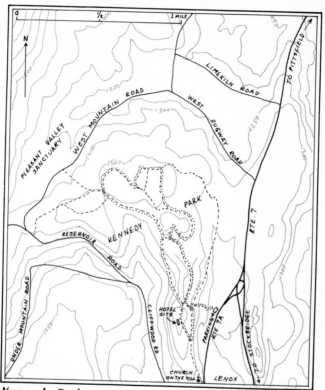

Kennedy Park

Trail description: The John D. Kennedy Park lies on the property of the old Aspinwall Hotel, built in 1902 to accommodate the superrich and superpowerful who wanted to spend a short time in Lenox with their wealthy colleagues who had built immense summer "cottages" in the area. The hotel burned down in 1931; the property was taken over by the town in 1957 and transformed into a park to be enjoyed by all. The trails in the park are well maintained and well marked, ideally suited to an easy half-day of walking or ski touring.

Though a visit to Kennedy Park is not a "wilderness experience," once you get a few minutes away from the parking lot and the noise of traffic on Rte. 7, there is a real sense of privacy and seclusion. Motorized vehicles are not allowed in the park.

The trail starts at the west side of the parking lot, away from the highway. It is marked by dark orange diamonds. It begins to ascend gently within a few yards of the parking lot and soon passes under a power or telephone line. About a hundred yards past the power line, it comes to a T intersection at an old woods road. Go to the left here and continue to follow the orange blazes as the road makes an immediate right turn and merges with another road also marked by white triangles.

After about 200 yds., there is a 4-way intersection. Take the trail marked by the orange diamonds. After about 10 minutes this trail rejoins the trail marked by white triangles. Jog to the right here and cross the white triangle trail, picking up the orange diamond trail again as it heads off to the north again. Within a few hundred yards, you will come to a small wooden lookout shelter which looks out to the north. Continue on the orange trail as it leaves the lookout area heading to the east. Stay on the orange trail for about 30 minutes until it once again joins with the white diamond trail. There are many side trails along this stretch, so it is necessary to keep an eye out for and follow the orange blazes at every intersection.

When, after 30 minutes, the trails intersect, go to the left on the trail marked by white diamonds. Another 20 minutes or so walking along this trail will bring you back to the intersection where the two trails initially diverged. At this intersection you have three choices, not counting the trail you have just been on. Take the middle of the three and you will, within a couple of hundred yards, come to the foundation of the old hotel in a clearing on the right. Imagine waking up in a room that looked out on the view you now see. To the west is Lenox Mtn., to the southwest is Stockbridge Mtn., and beyond are the Taconics—all providing a lovely backdrop for a leisurely breakfast or afternoon tea.

After this sojourn, double back to the 4-way intersection and this time turn hard right, following both the orange and white blazes. The orange-blazed trail turns off to the left after a couple of hundred yards, crosses the old woods road, and then falls off to the right towards the power line and the parking lot.

Pleasant Valley

Territory: Pleasant Valley Wildlife Sanctuary in Lenox.
Trail Length: Approximately 3 miles.
Start: Parking area at entrance to sanctuary on West Mountain Road.
Finish: Same.
Highest Point: Fire tower on Lenox Mountain (2126 feet).
Vertical Rise: 875 feet.
Time Estimate: 2½ hours.
USGS Quadrangle: Pittsfield West.

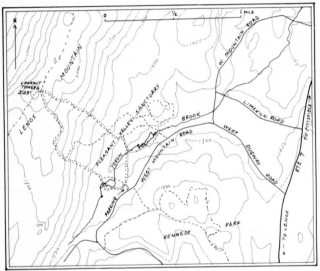

Pleasant Valley

Walking Trails

Directions to trailhead: From Lenox and the south, follow Rte. 7 or 7A going north. One-half mile after 7 and 7A merge, look for a gravel road turning off to the left. The road, W. Dugway Rd., is almost directly across from the Holiday Inn, and is marked by a sign for the sanctuary. Follow W. Dugway for about ¾ mi. where it joins West Mountain Rd. at a triangle. Turn left onto W. Mountain Rd. and follow it another ¾ mi. to the sanctuary entrance.

From Pittsfield and the north, follow Rte. 7 south towards Lenox and look for the Holiday Inn, just about 2 mi. south of the Pittsfield-Lenox town boundary. Across from the inn, turn right onto W. Dugway Rd. and follow directions above.

Trail description: The Pleasant Valley Sanctuary, one of 16 similar sanctuaries across the state maintained by the Massachusetts Audubon Society, is as well organized as any nature area in Berkshire County. The sanctuary has a museum, organized field trips, and some 20 trails covering every manner of typical Berkshire topography. The trail described below was chosen since it takes you through fields, over brooks and ponds, and also to the top of Lenox Mtn., where a panoramic view gives out onto the surrounding area including the sanctuary itself. The trails are well marked with blue blazes indicating trails that are heading away from the parking area, yellow blazes indicating trails returning. White blazes denote cross trails. There is an admission charge of $1.00 for use of the sanctuary, and, so as not to disturb the large resident population of wildlife, no dogs are allowed on the property.

From the parking lot, walk past the office and the museum on your right and look for the Bluebird Trail (or Lane) sign. At the end of the field, the trail enters the woods and immediately crosses Yokun Brook via a small wooden footbridge. Go straight ahead here, following the blue blazes. The trail soon crosses a second brook and comes to another intersection 20 yds. later. Go right here and follow the blue blazes until the trail comes to a T at the Old Wood Rd. Turn to the left here and continue to follow the blue blazes as the trail begins a mild ascent and parallels a small brook. The Old Wood Rd. soon comes to a 4-way intersection. Go straight ahead, again following the blue blazes, on the Overbrook Trail.

Once on the Overbrook Trail there are no more turns and the blue blazes continue. The ascent gets fairly steep and the trail crosses the brook several times. At times you may lose sight of the blazes for a moment or two, but there is always one nearby. If you do lose the blazes, do not wander off the trail assuming you know which way it heads. Stop or retrace your steps to the last blue blaze and then scan the trees for the next one.

Eventually, after a walk that may take an hour if you stop to catch your breath a couple of times, the trail emerges at the base of the fire tower atop Lenox Mtn. If the fence around the tower is unlocked, climb the stairs to get an even better view than the one from ground level. Do so, however, at your own risk. There was a time when this tower and ones like it throughout the county were manned nearly full time. The increased use of the airplane for spotting fires has led to the obsolescence of the towers, and they have become, to some minds, safety hazards. They are not kept up, and accidents can occur. It is sad that the airplane has taken over, since it was once enjoyable and informative to visit with the forest rangers as they surveyed the woodlands around them.

To return to the parking area, follow the Trail of the Ledges—marked with yellow blazes—which heads off to the southeast from the summit. In some spots the descent is a bit steep, but only for short stretches. In two or three spots it emerges from dense woods onto small ledges from which there are pleasant overlooks to the east. There is one intersection between the summit and the ledges, but it is easy

to miss. If you do come upon it, stay to the right and continue to follow the yellow blazes.

After about 40 minutes, the trail comes to a T intersection with the Nature Trail just short of a couple of beaver ponds. Go either left or right here and follow the Nature Trail, a loop beginning and ending at the sanctuary office next to the parking lot.

Tower Mountain Via The Skyline Trail

Territory: Pittsfield State Forest.
Trail Length: 13 miles (or 9 miles if you leave a second car at Pittsfield State Forest parking lot).
Start: Turnout on the north side of Route 20.
Finish: Same (or parking lot at Pittsfield State Forest).
Highest Point: 2193 feet.
Vertical Rise: 700 feet.
Time Estimate: 7 hours (or 5 hours if you choose the two-car option).
USGS Quadrangle: Pittsfield West.

Directions to trailhead: From the center of Pittsfield, follow Rte. 20 west towards New Lebanon, New York. After 4½ mi., Rte. 41 turns off Rte. 20 to the left (south). Stay on Rte. 20 as it passes the Shaker Village on the left within a few hundred yards of the intersection with Rte. 41. The turnout off Rte. 20, which is the parking area for the start of this walk, is 2¼ mi. past the Shaker Village on the right.

Trail description: This walk follows the route of the Taconic Skyline Trail which runs some 15 miles from the southern

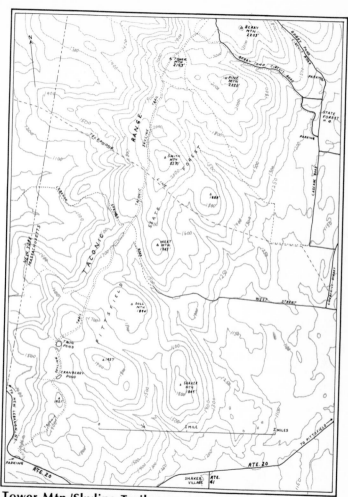

Tower Mtn./Skyline Trail

border of Pittsfield State Forest (Rte. 20) along the spine of the Taconic Range to the northern border of the forest at Potter Mountain Rd. The trail has not been kept up too well in recent years, although it is used frequently by walkers, trail bike riders, and snowmobilers. In some places it is a simple footpath, but most of the trail runs along a woods road that is known as the Taconic Fire Trail by state forest officials. Here and there faded white blazes may be spotted. For the most part, however, the trail is unmarked.

From the turnout on Rte. 20, walk back towards Pittsfield for a few yards and look for the beginning of the trail on the left (north) side of the highway. As of late 1978, there was a sign reading "Taconic Skyline Trail." The woods road climbs steadily away from the highway and towards the north. In several spots there are short detours where jeep drivers have created new tracks in order to bypass washouts. Now and again you might spot a small footpath merging with the woods road. In every instance, stay on the main track.

After about 1½ mi., the trail comes to a T. Turn right (east) at this intersection, and within 200 yds. pass a small pond off to the right of the trail. Within another 10 minutes the trail passes immediately alongside a larger pond. Overflow water trickles out of this pond heading towards the northwest. Just past this tiny stream the trail forks. Stay to the right here and follow along the woods road for another mile until the trail emerges into a clearing that runs along a low, rounded ridge. Here another woods road comes into the clearing from the west. Disregard it. The trail leaves the clearing heading northeast and passes through a stand of spruce trees that are apparently thriving here and well on their way to becoming twice as tall as they now are.

The trail continues along to the north for another half-hour until it comes to a 4-way intersection with a more traveled dirt road running northwest-southeast at the crossing. Cross this back road, known as Lebanon Springs Rd., and continue along the Skyline Trail which heads northeast from this intersection. Within 15 minutes, the trail crosses a narrow straight clearing which runs northwest-southeast. This section of the trail is marked sparingly by white blazes.

Bear left at a fork in the trail 1 mi. after crossing Lebanon Springs Rd. Within another ½ mi. there is another fork; bear right here and follow the white blazes. The trail comes to a T ½ mi. after this last fork. The more heavily traveled woods road goes to the right (east) at this T. Turn to the left here and follow a trail which soon becomes narrow, overgrown, and steep. Stay to the right at an intersection within a couple of hundred yards. Though they are hard to see, white paint blazes mark this section of the trail which dwindles quickly to a washed-out footpath. The grade is fairly steep here, but within 5 minutes it levels off and the trail emerges onto the broad, cleared summit of Tower Mtn. Here there are uninterrupted views to the south and west. Follow the trail through low brush to the northeast into another clearing with fine views to the north and west. If the weather is mild, this is the ideal spot for a picnic.

The summit of Tower Mtn. is also the half-way point in the walk, unless you brought along two cars and left one of them at the parking area at Pittsfield State Forest. If you did not bring two cars, retrace your steps down from the mountaintop and pick up the woods road again—this time heading to the south. Cross Lebanon Springs Rd. after 2½ mi. and continue along to the south on the Skyline Trail. Stay to the left at every intersection on the way back; within 2 hours the trail emerges onto Rte. 20 within spitting distance of the turnout-parking area.

If you left a second car at the state forest parking area, follow the white-blazed trail off the summit and into the underbrush heading northeast. The trail makes a short steep descent here for about 5 minutes until it rejoins the woods road from which it parted 10 minutes to the south side of the summit. This section is marked by white blazes, but they are faded, and few and far between. Keep a sharp eye out for them. If you lose track of the blazes, a short bit of bushwhacking may be in order. Follow your compass due east and you will come out on the woods road within 5 minutes. However you manage to regain the woods road, turn left once you are back on it. The road heads towards the northeast in this section. Within 10 minutes there is a 4-way intersection. Turn right here onto a footpath that heads downhill from the intersection towards the southeast. Within 5 minutes this path emerges onto a paved road, the southern leg of Berry Pond Circuit Rd.

Turn to the right on the paved road and begin a steady descent, leading to a fork in the road after an easy 20-minute walk. Bear right at the fork and pass a picnic area on the right. Within another 10 minutes the road comes to the parking area near the State Forest Headquarters.

Honwee Mountain

Territory: Pittsfield State Forest.
Trail Length: 4 miles.
Start: Parking area at the foot of Berry Pond Circuit Road.
Finish: Same.
Highest Point: 2313 feet.
Vertical Rise: 1040 feet.
Time Estimate: 2½ hours.
USGS Quadrangles: Hancock and Pittsfield West.

Directions to trailhead: From the center of Pittsfield, go west on West St. for 2½ mi. Turn right (north) onto Churchill St.

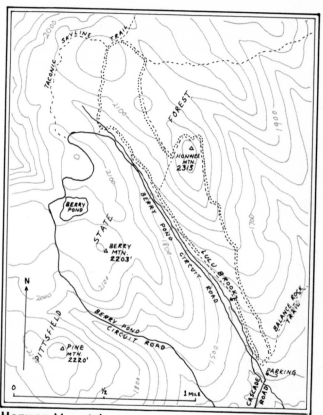

Honwee Mountain

and follow Churchill for 1¾ mi. Turn left at a sign for Pittsfield State Forest. After another ½ mi., turn right onto Cascade Rd. and enter the state forest within ½ mi. After stopping at the gate and paying the $2.00 entrance fee (no charge between October 15 and April 15), go straight ahead past State Forest Headquarters on the left. Within ¼ mi., there is a picnic and parking area on the left across from a small brown cabin. Park here.

Trail description: This walk takes you to and from the top of Honwee Mtn.—the tallest of several Taconic summits in Pittsfield State Forest. Honwee, along with Smith, Berry, Pine, and Tower mountains, surrounds Berry Pond—one of the highest bodies of water in the state. Unfortunately there is no view from the top of Honwee since the summit is broad and flat and is overgrown with assorted hardwoods. But the walk is a pleasant one. Do not shy away from Pittsfield State Forest simply because it is close to the city of Pittsfield.

From the parking area, cross Berry Pond Circuit Rd. and look for an orange triangle marking a woods road that starts into the forest between the brown cabin and a small bridge which takes the paved road over Lulu Brook. The trail climbs steadily but gradually towards the northwest and parallels the brook which is on the left. After ¼ mi., another woods road leads off to the right of the main trail. Go straight ahead here and continue to walk along for another 1½ mi. (30 minutes) until there is a similar intersection where another woods road turns off to the right. Go straight once again and stay with the trail until it comes to a T after another 10 minutes. From this intersection, Lulu Brook is to the left about 30 yards away. Turn right (towards the northeast) here and head away from the brook. Here again the trail is in the form of an old woods road.

Within ½ mi., a footpath merges with the woods road from the left. This trail is part of the Taconic Skyline Trail and is marked by white blazes. Stay on the woods road as it meanders towards the north. Within 10 minutes of the intersection with the white-blazed trail, an unmarked trail turns off the main trail and heads southeast. Turn onto this trail and follow it as it begins a gentle descent. After about 10 minutes on this trail, look for another unmarked trail which turns off to the right and heads southwest from the intersection. This trail winds and climbs over a shallow ridge and after 10 minutes comes to another T.

Turn left onto another trail which leaves the T intersection heading northeast. Stay to the right after about 5 minutes when another trail goes off to the left. The trail continues to climb for a few hundred yards until it eventually passes over the broad, flat summit of Honwee Mtn. You may not know that you have been across the summit until you notice that the trail has begun to descend gradually some 10 minutes after the last intersection.

From the top of Honwee, the trail descends steadily for 1½ mi. until it emerges onto the paved Circuit Rd. within a few yards of the brown cabin and across from the parking area. There are a couple of trails which turn off this last leg of the walk; bear or turn right at every opportunity.

Notchview

Territory: Notchview Reservation in the town of Windsor.
Trail Length: 5½-6 miles.
Start: Parking lot next to Budd Visitor Center.
Finish: Same.
Highest Point: Judges Hill (2297 feet).
Vertical Rise: 450 feet.
Time Estimate: 3 hours.
USGS Quadrangle: Windsor.

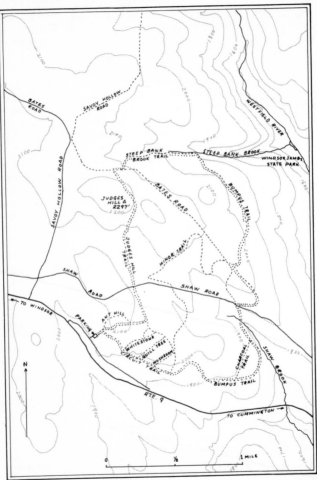

Notchview Reservation

Walking Trails

Directions to trailhead: From Pittsfield and the west, take Rte. 9 (also Rte. 8A once you get through Dalton) east heading for Windsor and Northampton. When 8A turns off to the left at Windsor, check the odometer in your car. The turnoff for Notchview is on the left exactly 1 mi. after the junction of Rtes. 9 and 8A.

From Northampton and east, follow Rte. 9 to the intersection of Rtes. 9 and 8A in Windsor. Turn around at this intersection and to back along Rte. 9 1 mi. to the entrance to Notchview on the left (north) side of the road.

Trail description: Notchview Reservation covers 3,000 acres and is the largest single holding of the Trustees of Reservations, the largest private landholder of conservation lands in the state. The reservation is clothed in assorted hardwoods and spruce, the latter an example of the reforestation that took place when old fields were abandoned. In the valleys and at lower elevations, white pines were apt to be the first evergreens to catch on when a farmer ceased to cultivate a field. In Windsor and other towns along the Berkshire Barrier that are up at least 1500 ft., spruce trees were the first to reclaim the fields.

The trustees have laid out an extensive network of trails on the reservation and provide, for $.20, a fine map detailing the trails. As of late 1978, admission to the reservation was $.50. From the map you can choose any number of trails; there is something to suit almost any appetite. The trail described below was selected only because it is the longest loop available. Other trails are, therefore, shorter but no less interesting.

From the parking lot, follow a sign that reads simply "Trail." Just after you enter the woods, there is an intersection marked with a sign reading "Circuit Trail." Turn to the right here and head up the Circuit Trail at 80°. There is an immediate but short climb here, and the trail is somewhat overgrown. It is marked with yellow blazes.

A 15-minute walk will take you past the Whitestone, Quill Tree, and Mushroom trails on the left, a large shed on the right, and to the border of a large field. Follow the road, heading 90°, into the middle of the field, passing an old cellar hole and a weathered barn on the right. The road peters out in the field, but the trail is now marked by single fence posts with a white band around the tip and the yellow blaze on the white. These fence posts take you to the southeast corner of the field where the trail reenters the woods heading 140°.

You are now on the Bumpus Trail which makes a loop to the east and comes back to the northwest along Shaw Brook. The trail eventually crosses the brook and climbs to intersect with Shaw Rd., a gravel town road open to anybody for any kind of use. You may be surprised here by a car going by — a rude interruption after the tranquility of the walk so far. Cross Shaw Rd. and pick up Bumpus Trail again on the other side, now heading off at 70°. After a couple of minutes the trail enters a large cleared area which was once the site of the Bates home. Here again the trail follows single white-and yellow-topped fence posts as it makes its way off to the north. This is the last large clearing on the trail, so if you are looking for a picnic site with a view, this will be your best bet.

At the north edge of the field, turn to the right and follow the fence posts into the woods again, this time past a sign that warns against ski touring on this section of the trail. The reason for the warning becomes obvious soon after as the trail crosses some pretty rough country on its way to, and then along, Steep Bank Brook. It is about a 20-minute walk from the field down to the brook, where you should turn to the left and begin to climb back up again for another 20 minutes until reaching a T at Bates Rd. Turn to the right on Bates Rd. and look for a trail to the left as you walk towards the west. This trail off to the left will be Judges Hill Trail and is within a couple of hundred yards of the spot where Steep Bank Brook Trail emerges onto Bates Rd.

Judges Hill Trail passes over the shoulder of its namesake, Judges Hill. Fifteen minutes later, approximately, it crosses Shaw Rd. which is still in gravel at this point. A few hundred yards past Shaw Rd., Judges Hill Trail merges with the Circuit Trail. Take your first right onto the Ant Hill Loop which will lead you, after about 10 minutes, back to the intersection near the parking lot from which you started your walk.

Greylock Loop

Territory: Mt. Greylock State Reservation.
Trail Length: 9½ miles.
Start: Parking area off Rockwell Road at Jones Nose.
Finish: Same.
Highest Point: Mt. Greylock (3490 feet).
Vertical Rise: 1700 feet.
Time Estimate: 5 hours.
USGS Quadrangles: Cheshire and Williamstown.

Directions to trailhead: From Pittsfield and south, follow Rte. 7 north towards Lanesborough and Williamstown. Turn off Rte. 7 to the right onto N. Main St. 1½ mi. north of the center of Lanesborough. Follow N. Main for ¾ mi. until it comes to a small triangle. Turn right (east) at the triangle onto Quarry Rd. Bear left onto Rockwell Rd. at a fork ½ mi. up Quarry Rd. A little over ½ mi. from the fork at Quarry Rd., there is a Visitor Center for the reservation with a knowledgeable and helpful staff. On leaving the Visitor Center, turn right and follow Rockwell Rd. as it climbs up the

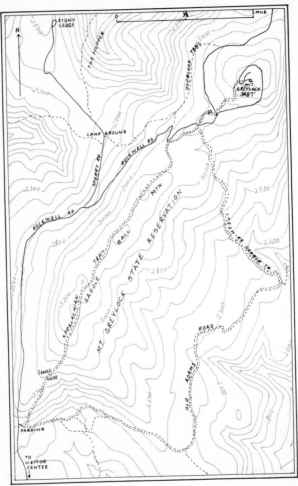

Greylock Loop

ridge of the Greylock Range. After 4 mi., look for a clearing on the right which serves as a parking area. No overnight parking is allowed.

From Williamstown and north, follow Rte. 7 south to Lanesborough. Turn off to the left onto N. Main St. and follow directions above. If you have any trouble finding N. Main St., go to the center of Lanesborough village, turn around, follow Rte. 7 north for 1½ mi. and look for N. Main on the right.

Trail description: As of early 1979, plans were being formulated to relocate a portion of the Appalachian Trail immediately north of the parking lot at Jones Nose. The proposed changes have not, as of this writing, been carried out, but it is expected that they will be in the near future. Check in at the Visitor Center to find out if the changes have been made; if they have ask for the new route of the trail. The proposed rerouting will only affect the first mile of this walk.

As the trail leaves the parking area and heads north, it passes through a heavy wooden barricade meant to keep out motorized vehicles. This first leg of the walk follows a section of the Appalachian Trail which is marked by white rectangles on end. The *Appalachian Trail Guide: Massachusetts-Connecticut* provides detailed information about the trail's route through Berkshire County and is available in libraries, bookstores, and sporting goods stores, or from the Appalachian Trail Conference, P.O. Box 236, Harpers Ferry, WV 25425.

Immediately after the barricade, the trail begins a steep climb to the north through an open area from which there are fine views to the south, east, and west. This climb up Jones Nose will give a quick indication of what kind of shape you are in. If you reach the top breathing easily, you are doing fine. If you are suffering, you are like most of us — out of shape. Do not hesitate to take a breather here even though you are still within sight of the parking area. There is a lot of climbing ahead, and there is no point in going at it with a sweat-soaked body and aching lungs.

Once the trail passes over Jones Nose and heads north towards Saddle Ball Mtn., it is covered on both sides by vegetation and there is a disappointing lack of overlooks. The only indication that you are walking along a ridge that connects three of the highest mountains in the Berkshires is the flora which suggests more northerly latitudes.

About ¾ mi. past Jones Nose, the trail passes over the south summit of Saddle Ball Mtn. (3238 ft.), but you may not know it because of the dense growth. Just before this first summit there is a fine overlook to the south and west; it is a few yards to the left (west) of the trail and could use some brush clearing if it is going to stay attractive for long. Within a few hundred yards of Saddle Ball, the trail passes through a spruce and balsam bog that may be hard to negotiate without getting your feet wet. The location of this bog seems improbable: considering the elevation, how is it that the water does not run off?

After the trail emerges from the bog, it continues along to the north for another 1¼ mi. Here it comes out onto Rockwell Rd. Turn to the right immediately and follow the trail back into the woods as it heads north once again. Within a few hundred yards it rejoins Rockwell Rd. at the northern terminus of the Cheshire Harbor Trail, which merges here from the southeast.

The trail (still marked by white blazes) crosses Rockwell Rd. at this point and begins a steep climb to the north. There is a brief flat stretch after a few minutes when the trail passes along the south side of a small pond. Fifty yds. past the pond the trail once again meets Rockwell Rd., this time at a 3-way intersection. Cross the intersection to the north side and pick up the footpath again. Ten minutes later the trail passes a television transmitting tower and enters the

Walking Trails

parking area which services the summit of Mt. Greylock. After a couple of hours of silence and solitude in the woods, it is a bit disappointing to find yourself in a crowd of cars and people, but the view from the top of Greylock is worth the aggravation.

On a clear day nearly all of the Berkshires and some of the Catskills, Adirondacks, and Green Mountains are visible. A special treat may be in store if the wind is from the east. Hang-glider devotees have discovered that the ledge just east of the Memorial Tower is a good launching pad for rides that take them well out over the Hoosac Valley and the city of Adams. It takes your breath away to watch these birdmen hurl themselves off the top of the mountain, as they first run down the ledge under ungainly looking rigs, then catch an updraft and shove off for a swooping, soaring ride that makes you stare at them in awe or horror—maybe both. The flight of the hang-gliders serves as a vivid counterpoint to the hours you have spent trudging up the mountain and the hours still ahead of you on the trip back to the parking area at Jones Nose.

If the weather is mild, the summit is a fine place for a picnic. Since there is almost always a breeze blowing, however, you might want to find a more protected spot.

Begin the descent back to Jones Nose by retracing your steps down the Appalachian Trail until it merges with the Cheshire Harbor Trail. Here you have a choice. If you cannot stand the sight of trail bikes or jeeps, you should go back down the Appalachian Trail the way you came up. Otherwise, try the Cheshire Harbor Trail for a little variety. This trail is an old woods road which is a bit washed out in some spots, but is easier walking than the Appalachian Trail.

After about 1½ mi. of steady, but never steep, descent, the Cheshire Harbor Trail intersects with another woods road called Old Adams Rd. Turn right (south) here onto Old Adams and follow it as it winds along the east shoulder of the Greylock Range. Bear right (west) at a fork after 1¾ mi. From this fork it is about 1½ mi. back to the parking lot from which you started up the Appalachian Trail. There are a couple of trails that join the Old Adams Rd. from the left along this stretch. Wherever there is a choice, turn or bear to the right.

Stony Ledge Loop

Territory: Mt. Greylock State Reservation.
Trail Length: 4½ miles.
Start: Campground on Sperry Road.
Finish: Same.
Highest Point: 2580 feet.
Vertical Rise: 1400 feet.
Time Estimate: 2½-3 hours.
USGS Quadrangle: Williamstown.

Directions to trailhead: From Pittsfield and south, follow Rte. 7 north towards Lanesborough and Williamstown. Turn off Rte. 7 to the right onto N. Main St., 1½ mi. north of the center of Lanesborough. Follow N. Main for ¾ mi. until it comes to a triangle. Turn right (east) at the triangle onto Quarry Rd. Bear left onto Rockwell Rd. at a fork ½ mi. up Quarry Rd. Follow Rockwell Rd. for 6½ mi. from this fork to another fork. Bear left here onto Sperry Rd. Park at the campground ½ mi. down Sperry Rd.

From the center of North Adams, follow Rte. 2 west for a little over 1 mi. Look for Notch Rd. on the left and a sign for Mt. Greylock Reservation. Turn left onto Notch Rd. Once you are on Notch Rd., make a sharp left after 1 mi. and a sharp right after 2 mi. From here Notch Rd. twists and turns

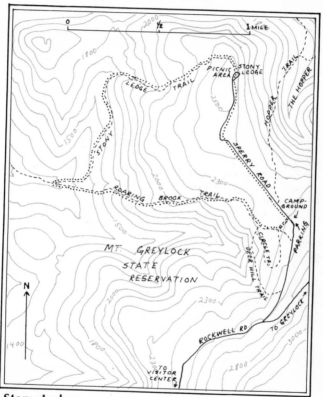

Stony Ledge

its way to within ¼ mi. of the summit of Mt. Greylock, where it comes to a T with Rockwell Rd. Turn right here onto Rockwell and drive 1½ mi. until Sperry Rd. doubles back to the right. Turn right onto Sperry and look for the parking area at the campground after ½ mi.

Trail description: This walk takes you to Stony Ledge via a steep descent along Roaring Brook Trail and then an equally steep climb up Stony Ledge Trail. The first leg will test the muscles in your legs, the second will test your lungs. Though the walk is not all that long, frequent breathers are recommended for those who are not in prime condition.

Leave the campground heading to the southwest and look for signs for Roaring Brook Trail. The trail immediately crosses a footbridge to the west side of the brook. Turn right 20 yds. after the bridge at a sign for Roaring Brook Trail. Within 150 yds. there is another fork in the trail just after another footbridge. Walk straight ahead onto Roaring Brook Trail which heads away from this intersection at 320°. From here the trail descends steadily, and in some places steeply, for about 1½ mi. where it intersects with the Stony Ledge Trail on the right. At this junction, Roaring Brook is right alongside the trail on the left. If the weather is warm this is a pleasant spot to rest, picnic, and cool your feet. Do not overeat, since there is a steep climb ahead of you.

Start up Stony Ledge Trail which heads a little south of east from the fork with Roaring Brook Trail. There is a sign at the foot of the trail which informs you that the trail is an intermediate ski trail. This trail is a part of the Mt. Greylock Ski Club system. It was not so long ago that dedicated skiers climbed this trail on foot.

The climb to Stony Ledge will take at least 45 minutes and maybe a good deal longer if you are out of shape and need to stop often to catch your breath. The view from the ledge makes the climb worthwhile, although it is somewhat disappointing, after all the work that you have done to get there, to be joined by people piling out of cars within a few feet of the overlook. From the ledge there is a fine view of the Hopper, a glacial cirque described in the chapter on geology, and the west face of Mt. Greylock.

To return to the parking area at the campground, follow the gravel road south from Stony Ledge. The campground is just over a mile away.

Berlin Mountain

Territory: Taconic Range in Williamstown along New York/Massachusetts border.
Trail Length: 4½ miles.
Start: Parking area at Williams College Ski Area.
Finish: Same.
Highest Point: Berlin Mountain (2798 feet).
Vertical Rise: 1300 feet.
Time Estimate: 3 hours.
USGS Quadrangle: Berlin, New York.

Directions to trailhead: From the intersection of Rtes. 2 and 7, 2¼ mi. south of the center of Williamstown, turn onto Rte. 2 heading west towards Taconic Trail State Park and Petersburg, New York. As Rte. 2 begins immediately to climb to the west, look for a small road off to the left just over ¼ mi. from the intersection of Rtes. 2 and 7. This is Torrey Woods Rd. and is marked by a sign reading "Carmelite Novitiate." Turn left here onto Torrey Woods and follow it towards the west. Oblong Rd. turns off to the left (south) after ½ mi. Continue along straight ahead on Torrey Woods to a fork ¾ mi. past Oblong Rd. Bear left at the fork and

Berlin Mountain

Walking Trails

drive another 1¼ mi. to the field and parking lot at the end of the road.

Trail description: While a large portion of this trail is actually in New York State, it is included in this collection because of the beautiful vista from the top of Berlin Mtn. All of the walking is along old woods roads and is nowhere difficult, although there is a healthy amount of climbing involved. Because this area is very popular with hunters during deer season, it should be avoided at those times. In Massachusetts, deer season is traditionally the first week in December. Check with local sporting goods stores to find out the dates of the hunting season in New York.

From the parking area, follow an old road that exits the field at the eastern end of the north border of the clearing. Here, just after the road enters the woods, turn to the left and begin to climb up towards Berlin Pass. The road is not blazed, but, aside from one side road leading off to the north after ¾ mi., there are no turns between the field and the pass. After about ¼ mi., look for a short stone pillar on the right of the trail; this post marks the state boundary.

This rutted track was at one time the Boston to Albany Post Rd. In the old days it seems that those responsible for laying out roads were apt to choose the shortest distance between two points without regard for the elevation or pitch in between. They could make tight turns when they had to, whereas today, given high-speed travel, engineers need more room to construct broad gentle turns in the roadway.

The old Post Rd. emerges from the woods onto Berlin Pass 1 mi. up from the beginning of the trail. Straight ahead the road descends into the town of Berlin, New York. To the right (north) there is a jeep track which follows the ridge line towards Petersburg Pass. Turn left onto the jeep track that heads south towards the summit of Berlin Mtn., 1¼ mi. away. There are fine views from the flat open area around the pass, but nothing like those that await you at the top of the mountain. It is about a 30-minute walk from the pass to the mountaintop, and in some places the trail is steep enough to make you wish that you were in better shape.

There is not much that you cannot see from the top of Berlin Mtn. To the east there is a great view of the Greylock Range; to the south lie the Taconics; and to the west you can see well into New York State with the Catskills and the Adirondacks in the background.

From Berlin Mtn. you can either retrace your steps to Berlin Pass and then descend to the parking lot by the same trail you climbed up, or, if you want to save a little time, walk to the northeast edge of the summit to find a trail into the woods which is blocked by a cable (to keep cars from trying to descend the ski slope ahead) within a hundred yards. On the other side of the cable is the top of the ski run which leads directly to the parking area in ¾ mi.

If you have time and energy to spare, you might want to explore the Taconic Crest Trail which heads southeast of the summit. This trail is marked by white blazes and eventually makes its way as far south as Rte. 43 in Hancock. For details about this section of trail, write to the Taconic Hiking Club, c/o R.H. Johnston, 50 Newark St., Cohoes, NY 12047.

Old Florida Road

Territory: Savoy Mountain State Forest.
Trail Length: 10 miles.
Start: Turnout on East Hoosac Street.
Finish: Same or North Pond parking area if you have two
 cars.
Highest Point: Spruce Hill—also known as Mt. Busby (2566

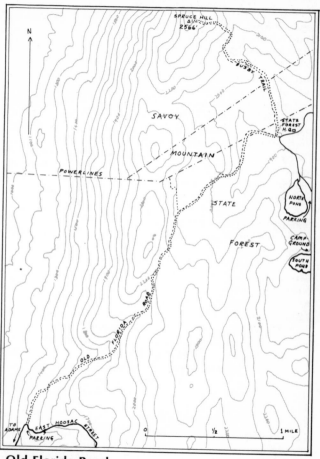

Old Florida Road

feet).
Vertical Rise: 1240 feet.
Time Estimate: 4 hours.
USGS Quadrangle: North Adams.

Directions to trailhead: In Adams, turn off Rte. 8 onto E. Hoosac St. which is on the opposite side of the street and 100 yds. north of the Public Library. Since the street is not well marked, it might be wise to stop and ask directions instead of wasting time looking for it. Once you have located E. Hoosac St., follow it past a large mill on the right and over a concrete sluice that channels the Hoosac River through the town. After ½ mi., E. Hoosac St. begins to climb through a residential area. One mi. from Rte. 8, E. Hoosac intersects with East Rd. Follow E. Hoosac across East Rd. where it beings to climb in earnest. Three-fourths mi. after the intersection with East Rd., there is a hairpin turn which switches back to the right. The start of the walk is on the left side of the road just at the turn. Park along the right side of E. Hoosac above the hairpin at one of the many turnouts. If you have two cars and wish to shorten this walk by about 3½ mi., take one car up to the parking area at the North Pond Recreation Area. To get there, follow E. Hoosac St.—which turns into Savoy Center Rd. without your knowing it—up the hill to the east. Three mi. from the hairpin turn, turn left onto Burnett Rd., the first road off of Savoy Center Rd. Follow Burnett for a little over a mile until it comes to a 3-way intersection. Turn left here onto Florida Rd. and follow it 2 mi. to the North Pond parking area. Leave one car here and return in the other to one of the turnouts just uphill from the hairpin turn.

Trail description: Walk down to the hairpin turn from your car and turn right off of E. Hoosac St. onto a rutted woods road that heads off to the north. This track is an abandoned

114

county road known as Old Florida Rd. The trail immediately begins a steady but gradual ascent. After about ½ mi. there is a pleasant view to the left (northwest) out over a field towards the Greylock Range. In the next mile there are two overgrown woods roads which merge with the trail from the south. Go straight ahead at both intersections.

The trail comes up on ledges of exposed bedrock just short of 2 mi. from E. Hoosac St. and begins to descend gradually once it passes these ledges. A swampy area just after the ledges may require a short detour in spring and early summer or after a heavy rain at other times of the year. While it may seem like a nuisance, remember that when it is wet it may discourage trail bike riders who like to use abandoned roads like this one. That the road was abandoned quite a while back becomes obvious after about 2 mi. Here erosion has chewed at the road with such persistence that the road has become a gully 6 ft. deep in some places. If you do not like walking in a ditch, there is a detour on the right which parallels the gully and rejoins it after a few hundred yards; the erosion here is not so bad. Shortly after the gully there is a level stretch from which an overgrown road turns off to the left (north). Walk straight ahead at this junction and follow the main trail for another ¾ mi. where it emerges from the woods to pass along the west side of a swamp. In the wet season you may have to cut up to the left here to avoid spongy footing.

At the far end of the swamp the trail passes under a power line and reenters the woods for a minute. Then it doubles back under the power line and within ¼ mi. emerges onto a paved road. Just short of the paved road, there is a trail going off to the left (north) which is marked by blue blazes. This is the Busby Trail which, after a distance of nearly 2 mi., leads to the summit of Spruce Hill (Mt. Busby). The trail is somewhat overgrown in places but never so much so that it is difficult to follow. At first it climbs gently, but after about

1 mi. the ascent becomes fairly steep as the trail heads north and then west towards the summit. The view from the top makes the struggle to get up the last couple of hundred feet worthwhile. The Hoosac Valley is at your feet, it seems, and on a clear day the eastern promontories of the Greylock Range appear to be within arm's reach. Those who like to watch migrating hawks in the fall find this a perfect vantage point. The birds glide by on billows of rising air heated in the valley below.

It takes about 45 minutes to return to the foot of the Busby Trail. If you left one car at the North Pond parking area, turn left at the foot of the trail and then right onto the paved road. From here it is less than ½ mi. to the parking area. If you must return to the start of the walk on E. Hoosac St., turn right at the foot of the Busby Trail and retrace your steps under the power line and then up and down the Old Florida Rd.

Borden Mountain

Territory: Savoy Mountain State Forest.
Trail Length: 8 miles (10 miles with side trip to Tannery Falls).
Start: Parking area at the corner of Burnett Road and New State Road.
Finish: Same.
Highest Point: Borden Mountain (2505 feet).
Vertical Rise: 1100 feet.
Time Estimate: 4-5 hours.
USGS Quadrangles: Windsor and North Adams.

Directions to trailhead: From Adams, take Rte. 116 east towards Savoy. After 7 mi., Rte. 116 intersects with Rte. 8A,

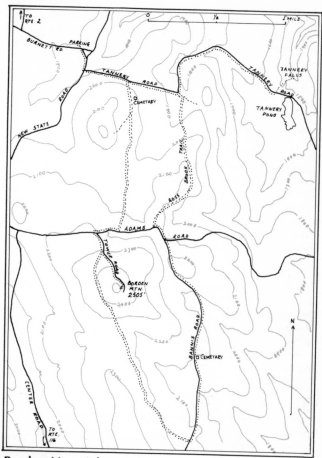

Borden Mountain

which turns off to the right and heads toward Windsor. Stay on 116 for another ½ mi., then turn left onto Center Rd. which is not well marked. A safer bet would be to continue on 116 for another few hundred yards and stop and ask directions to Center Rd. at the Savoy general store on the right side of the highway. Once you are on Center Rd., follow it for 3 mi. until it comes to a T intersection with Adams Rd. Go left onto Adams Rd., but only for a few hundred yards. Turn right onto New State Rd. Follow New State Rd. going north for 1 ¾ mi., past a road to the right heading for Tannery Falls, until New State Rd. comes to a 3-way intersection with Burnett Rd. Turn left onto Burnett. A hundred yards down Burnett will bring you to a large parking area on the right.

From the West Summit, go east along Rte. 2 for ½ mi. to Shaft Rd., which turns off to the right. From Whitcomb Summit, follow Rte. 2, 2 mi. to the west and turn left onto Shaft Rd. Once on Shaft Rd., follow it to the south and follow signs for North Pond picnic camping area and for Savoy Mtn. State Forest. Stay to the right at the first intersection, about ½ mi. down Shaft Rd. At the second intersection, 1 mi. after the first, go straight ahead. (On your left at this intersection, there is a fenced-in building with a couple of strange looking cones projecting out of one side. This is the central shaft for the Hoosac Tunnel. When the tunnel was being built, men were lowered down this shaft to dig from the center of the tunnel out to both ends. There was a small town at this site, where the workmen lived and from which they only had a one thousand foot trip to work every day. Given the crude elevator system and the horrible working conditions which faced them when they reached bottom, however, it cannot have been a pleasant trip.) Take the first right after the central shaft, about ½ mi. farther down the road. Stay on this road (still called Shaft Rd. until it crosses the Florida/Savoy town line when it becomes Florida Rd.) as it winds past the State Forest Headquarters and then the North Pond recreation and camping areas. After nearly 3 mi. the road intersects with Burnett Rd. at a T. To the right Burnett Rd. is gravel, and to the left it is hard-surfaced. Take the paved option to the left and look for the parking area on the left ½ mi. down Burnett.

Trail description: Walk back out onto Burnett Rd. and take a left, followed by an immediate (100 yds.) right onto New State Rd. which drops down and crosses a bridge over Gulf Brook within a few hundred yards. As the road climbs from the bridge, you will see a gravel road turning off to the left with signs for Tannery Falls. Turn left here and follow Tannery Rd. as it makes a long slow climb to the east. At the crest of the hill, after about ¼ mi. or 5 minutes walking, look for a trail going off the road to the right marked by orange blazes. Follow this trail as it heads south and within a couple of minutes passes by a lovely small cemetery on the left. You may find yourself wondering what a cemetery is doing out here in the boondocks, even if it is a quiet, secluded spot. A hundred and fifty years ago this area and areas like it up and down the Hoosac Range were the centers of activity in the Berkshires. All this area was farmed or logged or both, and the forest cover that now blankets the area was almost completely cleared.

After another 300-400 yds. there is a fork in the old woods road on which you are walking. Stay to the left here and continue along the woods road to the south until, after about a mile, it reaches Adams Rd.—a gravel, well-maintained county road. Turn to the right on Adams Rd. and walk along to the west past a paved road going off to the left. One hundred yds. after the paved road there is a fenced clearing on the right. There is a beautiful vista here to the northeast, out over the hills and mountains of Florida, Rowe, and Monroe and into southern Vermont. Though the field is an inviting spot to rest, it is private property and should not be entered.

Double back to the paved road that you just passed, which now turns off to the right (southeast) and begins to climb right away. Follow this road to the summit of Borden Mtn., ½ mi. away. The summit is nearly flat and trees have grown up around the fire and radio towers so that it is difficult to get a good view. The fire tower, like most of those

Walking Trails

still standing in Berkshire County, is no longer occupied, as airplane surveillance has taken over as the major means of forest fire detection.

After a rest stop at the summit of Borden, retrace your steps back down the hard-surfaced road for ¼ mi. until you spot a woods road doubling back to the left. This trail will take you to the south for about 35 minutes or 1½ mi. The walking here, as it is all along this hike, is easy with no steep pitches. The trail passes through thick stands of evergreens, where all of a sudden the forest is still. It also passes through a clearing which surrounds an old cellar hole and a few apple trees—another reminder that this area was once settled and not nearly as wild as it is today.

The trail eventually intersects with Bannis Rd., another well-maintained gravel road that runs roughly north-south. Turn left onto Bannis and follow it north for nearly 2 mi. or about 40 minutes. It passes by a couple of old stone dams and another family graveyard. Dams such as these were sprinkled along every brook in the county around 1800. They regulated the flow of water in the streams in order to power the saw and gristmills that kept the communities prospering.

When, after 2 mi., Bannis Rd. comes to a T with another gravel road, you are back on Adams Rd. and should turn to the left. Within 300 yds. there is a trail off Adams Rd. to the right. This trail is marked at its start by orange blazes and heads into the woods at 30°. It is known as Ross Brook Trail and is not particularly well marked, although it is not difficult to follow, being another old overgrown woods road. Stay on this trail for about 25 minutes and it will eventually emerge onto a gravel road that runs northwest-southeast. Take a left onto this road and follow it for 5 minutes until it intersects with Tannery Rd.

From here you can turn left and follow Tannery Rd. for ½ mi. until it intersects with New State Rd., where you should turn right then left after the bridge onto Burnett Rd. and back to the parking area. Or, you can turn right onto Tannery and follow it for about a mile to the parking area for Tannery Falls. After a visit to the falls, walk back out Tannery Rd. for 1½ mi. to New State Rd.

Monroe Loop

Territory: Monroe State Forest in the towns of Monroe and Florida.
Trail Length: Approximately 9 miles.
Start: Lower Dunbar Parking Area on River Road.
Finish: Same.
Highest Point: Spruce Mountain (2730 feet).
Vertical Rise: 1600 feet.
Time Estimate: 5-6 hours.
USGS Quadrangles: North Adams and Rowe.

Directions to trailhead: From Rte. 2 (Mohawk Trail), go east from Whitcomb Summit ½ mi. to Whitcomb Hill Rd. Turn left down Whitcomb Hill Rd. and turn right at a fork within a few hundred yards from Rte. 2. Follow Whitcomb Hill until it comes to a T at River Rd. Turn left on River Rd. and pass through the tiny town of Hoosac Tunnel, which was, during the building of the tunnel, a thriving community, although today you probably will not even realize that you are going through the town. After you have crossed the tracks leading to the tunnel, the Lower Dunbar parking area is 4¼ mi. up River Rd. You will pass the Visitor Center for the Bear Swamp Pumped Storage Project; this might be worth a visit after your hike. The parking area is on the left and not particularly well marked, but it is only ¾ mi. past the Visitor Center. Keep a sharp lookout for it.

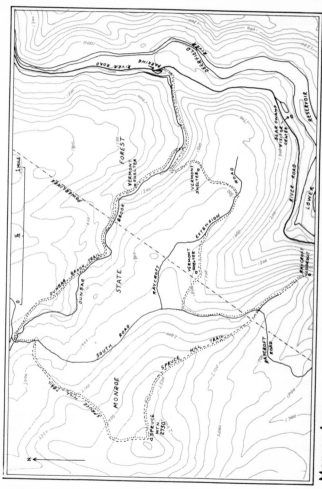

Monroe Loop

Trail description: The majority of this trail is for foot traffic only. It is very well maintained as of October 1978. There are sections of the trail which go along gravel country roads, and these no doubt see their share of snowmobile traffic in winter and other vehicles the rest of the year.

The trail leaves the parking lot at the southwest corner and heads off in a southerly direction. Within a few minutes, it heads west and parallels Dunbar Brook, lying to the north side of the trail. There is a gradual ascent during the first leg of the walk, just enough to get you loosened up. After 20 minutes the trail intersects with a trail leading off to the left that is marked by a sign reading "Raycroft Lookout," and with another trail that leads to a footbridge over Dunbar Brook. Take the left towards Raycroft Lookout.

This section of the trail is fairly steep and ought to get your lungs cleared out pretty quickly. After about 20 minutes, there is a "Vermont" shelter on the right of the trail, which can be used for overnight protection from the elements. Another 10 minutes past the shelter, the trail comes out on a gravel road, called Raycroft Extension Rd. Go left along this road for about 6 or 7 minutes or about ¼ mi. Keep an eye out for the foot trail going off to the left and marked by blue paint blazes. The trail turns off to the left after a couple of minutes and then to the right several minutes later after passing another shelter. After a few more minutes the trail passes under power lines which seem to crisscross the Berkshire landscape and, for a minute, might remind you that you are not really in the wilds at all, but this impression does not last long as the trail plunges back into the forest. Soon enough you will be reminded of man's determination to explore and develop anything that stands in his way when, after a few minutes, the trail comes out onto Raycroft Rd.

Go left onto Raycroft Rd. and follow it in a generally southeast direction for about 15 minutes until there is a

Walking Trails

3-way intersection. If you want to see the fine view from Raycroft Lookout, follow the road that continues towards the southeast for ½ mi., but bear in mind that you may be joined there by others who have come on the wings of the internal combustion engine.

After walking hard for more than an hour and a half, there is something slightly depressing about the odor of Detroit. And if you stay on the trail, there are other lookouts that are almost as pleasing and certainly more private. If you do choose to go to Raycroft Lookout, retrace your steps to the 3-way interesection mentioned above. From here the blue-blazed trail heads off to 310°. A sign reading "Spruce Hill Foot Trail" marks the beginning of this section of the trail.

After about 20 minutes on the Spruce Hill Trail, there is a fine overlook off to the left. This might be the perfect spot for a picnic, although this walk offers several special sites. Another 15 minutes along the trail will bring you to the summit of Spruce Mtn. Here, there is another fine vista off to the southeast. The white-spired church on Rte. 2 in the town of Florida can be seen on the far side of the valley.

From the summit of Spruce Mtn. follow the trail off to the north for 30 to 40 minutes until it rejoins Raycroft Rd. Turn left onto the gravel road and walk downhill for a few hundred yards past a small parking lot on the right, and then turn right onto another gravel road which immediately crosses over Dunbar Brook.

The foot trail goes off to the right within a few yards of the end of the bridge. It again is marked by the blue blazes. This leg of the walk starts off paralleling the brook, but within a few minutes the trail climbs to the north away from the brook and intersects with an old woods road. Go right onto the old road (still following the blue blazes) which soon peters out, then continue on the foot path; it soon regains the north side of the brook and then, for about 2 mi., follows the brook downstream.

The brook is one of the loveliest in the area. It is strewn with boulders of all sizes, which in turn have created pools of every description, many of which invite you to dip in them on a hot summer day. The vast amount and variety of the boulders is a testament to the power and perseverance of erosion. At one time, maybe millions of years ago, these rocks were settled comfortably at elevations much higher than where they are today. But as water first crept and then rushed around them, they were gradually undermined and settled further and further down into the valley that was being carved around them. Finally they find themselves at the bottom; but then they are really never at the bottom, since even today a stream such as Dunbar Brook is digging its way deeper into the valley, and the valley is constantly dropping lower and lower. For the meantime, however, the boulders present us with a stream that tumbles and wanders and is a delight to walk along.

Two mi. downstream from the start of this leg of the walk, the trail crosses the brook and meets up at the first intersection you came to at the start of the hike. Go left and retrace your steps along the initial leg back to the parking lot, about 20 minutes away.

While this hike is mostly outside the Berkshire County limits, it is a special one and deserves to be included in this collection. It has everything—plenty of time spent walking along the brook and along old country roads, several pleasant overlooks, and a healthy dose of wilderness foot trails, not to mention the Vermont shelters and camping areas that make the idea of spending the weekend in this state forest an inviting one. The Massachusetts Department of Environmental Management and the New England Power Company, who together have established and maintained this system of trails, deserve credit for a job well done.

Ski-Touring Trails

In the early part of the winter before the snows come, I find that I notice the cold more when I am indoors than when I am outside. I shiver listening to the depressing harmony of the north wind outside and the oil burner in the cellar. To fend off the chills, I huddle deeper into a snug corner trying to nurture some small kernel of warmth. I marvel at the wildlife that thrives in the winter, I envy those species that migrate, and I empathize with those that hibernate.

The temptation to hunker down and outlast the cold wins out for a while, but soon enough—usually by the middle of January—I notice a rebellion stirring within me. Complaints from a body that has been left unattended for too long bring me to my senses, finally, and I step outside, no matter how cold it is. Exercise and fresh air, I remember from winters past, are the only tonics which I know will dispel my winter doldrums. Dreams of sandy, sun-burned beaches vanish and I begin to get up in the morning feeling alive and glad of it. Judging by the popular response to cross-country skiing in the last few years, it is apparent that more and more of us are realizing that you do not have to suffer passively through the winter.

Twenty years ago, ski touring was largely unheard of. The few people who knew of the sport dismissed it as masochistic, most likely, or the crazed exhibitionism of a handful of fools who had cabin fever and wished that they had been named Stefan, Ingmar, or Ulf. Today, nearly everyone who has an interest in exercise and the outdoors has heard of ski touring, and most of us have tried it or would like to. And, whereas it was once difficult to find suitable equipment, there are now as many makes and models of touring skis as there are tennis racquets and running shoes.

Enthusiasm for cross-country skiing is in full bloom in Berkshire County. On a given Saturday in mid-winter there are probably as many people heading for back country trails as there are for downhill ski areas. Some downhill areas now offer rental equipment and trails for those who prefer to ski on level ground and even uphill. Areas that are devoted solely to cross-country skiing have sprung up across the county (a list of these areas appear at the end of this section). These ski-touring centers offer rentals, instruction, and either use of their own trails or directions to nearby trails in several state forests. Be advised that the state forests are also open to snowmobiles. Recognizing the fact that skiers and snowmobilers do not often mix well, the planners for the Massachusetts Department of Environmental Management are trying to sort our state forest trails for winter use. Their prime concern is with safety; they are worried about the possibility of an accident involving a snowmobile and one or more skiers.

Because the snowmobile craze preceded widespread interest in cross-country skiing, because the operator of a snowmobile must purchase a license from the Commonwealth, and because snowmobilers have organized themselves into clubs and know how to lobby, state forest officials have worked to accommodate their wishes. In most of the forests there are probably ten miles of snowmobile trails for every mile of ski trails. Nevertheless, an effort is being made to provide more and better trails for those of us who go into the woods on winter weekends looking for a respite from our dependence on modern miracles such as the internal combustion engine.

Where a state forest is divided into two sections — as at Sandisfield State Forest — or where there are at least two separate entrances, planners have no trouble segregating skiers and snowmobilers. Problems arise when all traffic into a state forest shares a common access, and when devotees of either sport disregard trails which have been set out exclusively for them and instead use any trail which suits them. Wider trails and roads are usually reserved for the use of snowmobiles; ski trails are most commonly laid out along narrower, more remote routes. The beginning skier often cannot resist the temptation to stay on the broad, open trails. Certainly there is less chance of colliding with a tree and also less chance of getting lost if you stay close to the beaten path. There is no official policy of patrolling state forest trails. You are on your own and cannot expect to be extricated from a messy or possibly dangerous situation at the end of the day.

For this reason, you should never ski alone in the state forests or in any other area where there is not some sort of "trail sweep" before dark. If you insist on breaking this rule of thumb, be absolutely sure that someone knows where you are going and when you expect to return. A night spent alone in the woods in the dead of winter is to be avoided at all costs unless, of course, you are equipped for it, which means carrying a tent, sleeping bag, stove, food, etc.

Equipment for a day's skiing can be carried in a small back or hip pack. Be sure to include a map, compass, extra layer of clothing, and, if you are going out for more than a couple of hours, something to eat and drink. Other items that do not weigh much and could be lifesavers include a first-aid kit, flashlight, whistle, pocketknife, and space blanket. Unless the weather is especially bitter, do not burden yourself with lots of heavy clothing. Since you are moving all the time while skiing, you will find that there is more often a problem of keeping cool rather than warm. It does not take long to start perspiring; drying sweat-soaked undergarments, on the other hand, seems to take forever and is definitely uncomfortable and sometimes dangerous. Much has been written recently about the dangers of hypothermia, which can overtake a skier or anybody else outdoors when the body cools faster than it can be warmed from within. You will not have a problem with hypothermia if you keep moving, as the body will keep up a steady supply of heat. If you stop suddenly in an exposed spot, however, and find yourself being chilled by bitter gusts of arctic air sweeping down from the northwest, you are inviting trouble. To guard against cooling off too quickly, carry a light wind-proof parka which you can slip on over other clothes. Once you regain the shelter of the forest or the warmth of movement, it does not take a minute to remove the outer layer.

Otherwise what you wear depends on your taste or your existing wardrobe. You can invest heavily in fancy skiing wear that will make you look and possibly feel like an international racer. For most of us, however, an old (or new) pair of jeans will suffice. Knickers, because they do not constrict the movement of your legs, are also very popular. When the temperature is below the freezing point, a pair of long johns is a must under whatever kind of outer pants you choose. Up top, I find myself most comfortable in a long-sleeved cotton undershirt covered by a heavy wool shirt and an insulated vest which I can remove and stuff in my small pack when I get too warm. Turtlenecks are favored by many, but I find that the tight neck tends to trap excess body heat which leaves me sweating before I want to. If I have to drive any distance after skiing, however, I always change into a turtleneck when I get back to the shelter of my car; there is nothing worse than driving home in a wet undershirt. A knitted wool cap will keep your head warm, although on cold, win-

Ski-Touring Trails

dy days you might think of carrying an insulated hood which can be detached from a heavy parka and worn independently. It will probably take a few trips before you discover what dress and equipment suits you best.

If you are new to ski touring, think of experimenting with different kinds of skis, boots, and poles by renting them. A well-stocked rental shop will offer wood, fiberglass, and waxless (either wood or fiberglass) skis. Wood skis are easy to wax and clean and seem to have a special feel about them, if only because it is easy to relate to the material from which they are made. In all likelihood they will be so expensive in a few years that they will no longer be marketed. Fiberglass skis are lighter and stronger (as a rule) than wood skis and make a good deal of sense if you plan to do most of your skiing in the boondocks where a broken ski could be a real inconvenience. Waxless skis save you the trouble—some consider it a pleasure—of worrying about snow conditions, but in most cases do not perform as well as properly waxed skis. Some salespersons, convinced that statistics sell skis, will cite all sorts of fancy data to back up their assertion that one ski is better—or worse—than the next. All you need to worry about is the length, width, and weight of the ski in question.

Although I will mention a few tips that can make life easier for you once you get on the trail, I am not an expert skier, and I will not presume to tell you how to ski. I recommend that you consider taking a lesson or two, if you are a beginner, and that you read any of several fine books on skiing. Many people consider John Caldwell's *Cross-Country Skiing Today* (Stephen Greene Press, 1977) to be the bible of the sport. With an average amount of coordination and persistence, you can learn to ski without help from anybody, but it never hurts to have some pointers from those who really know their business.

If you have never been on skis before, spend a couple of afternoons practicing on level ground before you tackle the trails described in this book. Although some of the trails—Canoe Meadows and Pleasant Valley, for example—are over nearly flat terrain, you can practice anywhere there is some open space and some snow. City parks, golf courses, and athletic fields are all possibilities. Once you have some confidence in your ability to get around on skis, you will want to learn how to climb a hill and then run down it. Skiing downhill means learning how to stop and turn, two techniques you should know about before you head out on most of the trails described in later pages. I have labeled three trails as novice and twelve as intermediate. Novice trails are very nearly level throughout and without many turns. Intermediate trails require proficiency in climbing, turning, and stopping. Check the vertical rise listed for each trail against the trail length to get a better idea of how steep a specific trail is.

It is a good idea to find out what kind of condition you are in before you venture out onto a trail which runs several miles into the forest. Keep your first few trips well within your range. Stay close to home if it is very cold or threatening to snow. Stay even closer if you are skiing alone.

When you come to a downhill stretch in a trail, use a snowplow to check your speed often enough to stay under control at all times. Do not go whistling around corners when you are unable to see what or who is around the bend. Do not hesitate to fall—even gracelessly—if you find yourself running along too quickly and cannot slow down using a snowplow. When a descent looks too steep to negotiate comfortably, take your skis off and walk.

While is is usually easier to ski in tracks than in unbroken snow, do not shy away from the latter. The going will be slower, of course, but it can turn out to be just as enjoyable, especially if the untrodden trail takes you and your companions to places where you will be alone.

If, as you drive through the Berkshires, you come across a

field or old woods road that looks inviting, make sure that you ask permission from the landowner before setting out. Some will welcome you onto their property, and some will not. There is no harm in asking and there is no excuse in not asking. All the trails described in this book run over public property or land which is open to the public but owned by non-profit organizations such as the Trustees of Reservations.

In addition to the trails described below, some of the walking trails described earlier in this book can be used for ski touring. If Ashley Hill Brook is frozen over, the trail to Alander Mountain—at least the lower portions of it—is suited to skiing. There are some very steep stretches on the way to Tower Mountain via the Skyline Trail, but they should not deter advanced skiers who are looking for an extended tour over beautiful country. Portions of the Greylock Loop—Old Adams Road and the Cheshire Harbor Trail—can be used in conjunction with the Rockwell Road ski trail. And while you are up on Greylock, you might want to try either the Stony Ledge or Roaring Brook trails, but be warned that both of these are steep.

Use your head, use your body, and use the opportunity to get outside and ski, ski, ski.

Ski-Touring Centers

BLACKBERRY RIVER INN: Rte. 44, Norfolk, CT 06058; phone 203-542-5614.

BUCKSTEEP MANOR: Washington Mt. Rd., Washington, MA 01223; phone 413-623-5535.

BUTTERNUT SKI TOURING: Rte. 23, Great Barrington, MA 01230; phone 413-528-0610.

CUMMINGTON FARM: South Rd., Cummington, MA 01026; phone 413-634-2111.

EGREMONT COUNTRY CLUB: Rte. 23, South Egremont, MA 02158; phone 413-528-4222.

EGREMONT INN: Rte. 23, South Egremont, MA 02158; phone 413-528-2111.

FLYING CLOUD INN: Star Rte. 70, New Marlborough, MA 01230; phone 413-229-2113.

FOXHOLLOW RESORT: Rte. 7, Lenox, MA 01240; phone 413-637-2000.

JUG END: South Egremont, MA 01258; phone 413-528-0434.

OAK 'N' SPRUCE: Rte. 102, South Lee, MA 01260; phone 413-243-3500.

OTIS RIDGE: Rte. 23, Otis, MA 01253; phone 413-269-4444.

RED FOX: S. Sandisfield Rd., New Marlborough, MA 01230; phone 413-229-7790.

RIVERRUN NORTH: Rte. 7, Sheffield, MA 01257; phone 413-528-1100.

STUMPSPROUTS: West Hill Rd., Charlemont, MA 01339; phone 413-339-4265.

SWISS HUTTE: Rte. 23, Hillsdale, NY 12529; phone 518-325-3333.

Ashley Hill Brook Trail
(Intermediate)

Territory: Mt. Washington State Forest.
Trail Length: 8 miles.
Start: Parking area behind Mt. Washington State Forest
   Headquarters.
Finish: Same.
Highest Point: 2150 feet.
Vertical Rise: 650 feet.
Time Estimate: 3 hours.
USGS Quadrangle: Bashbish Falls.

Directions to trailhead: From Great Barrington, follow Rte.
23 west towards South Egremont and Hillsdale, New York.
Just past the center of South Egremont, turn left (south) onto
Rte. 41. Within a few hundred yards and just after a swampy
pond to the right of the road, turn right onto Mt. Washington
Rd. Follow this road along a straight stretch for about 2 mi.
when suddenly the road plunges into the Taconic Range.
After the road passes the Egremont-Mt. Washington town
line, two roads turn off to the right. Bear left at the first intersection and turn left at the second, following signs for Mt.
Everett Reservation. Pass the entrance to the reservation on
the right (east) side of the road and continue on for another
¼ mi. to a 4-way intersection. Go straight ahead (south) here
along East St. The State Forest Headquarters is on the right
(west) side of the road 1 mi. after the intersection and about
50 yds. past the merger of East and West Streets. The parking
area is behind the brown garage that houses the headquarters.

Trail description: This trail takes you west from the State
Forest Headquarters into the heart of Mt. Washington State

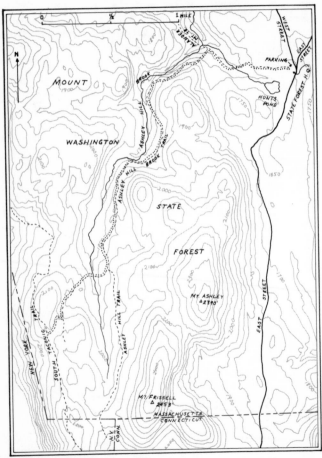

Ashley Hill Brook Trail

Ski-Touring Trails

Forest and the South Taconic Highland. Perhaps because the area is relatively inaccessible—especially during the winter months—there does not seem to be that much use of this state forest. Mt. Washington is one of the most sparsely populated and loveliest towns in the county; it is a jewel in the southern Berkshire landscape. Since there are few private homes in the vicinity and since there is little traffic on the trails here, take extra care when you use the trail described below. Make sure that you have let someone know where you are skiing and when you plan to return. If you have come some distance to ski here, check in with the personnel at the State Forest Headquarters and let them know of your plans. The office is open every day of the week between 8:30 a.m. and 4:30 p.m., although oftentimes the staff members are out plowing or clearing trails. You can pin a note on the door describing your route and estimated time of return.

From the parking area behind the garage, the trail heads west across a small field which is a perfect place to warm up if you have not been on skis for a while. On the far (western) side of the field the trail heads into the woods. A blue triangular marker here will help you find your way but there are very few of them further along the trail. Within a few hundred yards the trail emerges from the woods into another clearing and turns left and west once again. Here there is a nice descent for a few hundred yards. At the bottom of the clearing the trail angles to the left and then turns immediately to the right and passes a private dwelling. The trail then crosses Lee Pond Brook via a wooden bridge. From the bridge, the trail follows an old woods road which, after about ¼ mi., divides. Bear left at this intersection, following a sign reading Ashley Hill Brook Trail.

From the fork the trail swings away to the southwest and begins to climb gently. Here again the trail is an old woods road so that there is plenty of width, and, even though there

137

are no blazes, there is never any question about which way to go. Flat stretches offer regular relief from the climbing which is never arduous due to the gentle pitch of the trail. About 2 mi. from the fork a trail turns off to the left (southeast). This side trail is marked by a sign reading "Ashley Hill Trail." Continue along straight ahead towards the southwest. This next portion of the trail is open to snowmobiles, but there is reportedly very little traffic in this section of the forest.

Within ¼ mi. of the turnoff for the Ashley Hill Trail, the trail comes to a small clearing which is about 30 yds. across. On the far side of the clearing the trail makes a 90° turn to the right (northwest) and immediately crosses Ashley Hill Brook on a small wooden bridge. Once across the bridge, the trail swings to the southwest again and continues to climb easily towards another intersection about ¼ mi. away. This intersection was marked by orange triangles as of February 1979. Turn right (northwest) at this intersection and follow the trail, which is unmarked but obvious through this section, as it climbs gradually towards a ridge about ½ mi. away. You can tell that you are getting near the top of the ridge by the presence of laurel in the woods and by the stunted trees which never reach very grand heights up here where the wind is almost always blowing.

Once it passes the ridge, the trail drops suddenly to the west, but only for about 30 yds. when it comes to a T intersection with the South Taconic Trail, also known as the State Line Trail. The South Taconic Trail, which is well marked throughout by white blazes, straddles the New York-Massachusetts border as it runs from just south of the Connecticut-Massachusetts border north to Rte. 23 in Egremont. From this intersection, the very northwestern corner of Connecticut is only ¾ mi. away to the southeast, and the New York border is about 200 yds. to the west.

At this point, I turned around and skied back down to the

parking area by the route just described. You may wish to explore a bit up here, but I cannot vouch for the safety of the South Taconic Trail for skiing in this area. Further to the north—between Alander Mtn. and Bashbish Falls—the trail is steep and narrow in some places and is not suitable for skiing, especially where it drops down precipitously to Bashbish Falls. If you choose to investigate this trail either to the north or south, proceed cautiously.

If you are content to return from the ridge directly to the parking area and the start of this trail, take a few minutes to bushwack to the left (north) of the trail right at the ridgetop. Here there is a small bald spot from which there is a fine view of neighboring ridge lines and summits and a glimpse over into the Harlem River Valley in New York State to the southwest. If the weather agrees, this is a fine spot for a picnic break.

The run back to the parking lot is delightful and should take about half as long as it took to get up to the ridge.

Mt. Everett
(Intermediate)

Territory: Mt. Everett Reservation in the town of Mt. Washington.
Trail Length: 3½ miles.
Start: Parking lot just outside entrance gates to Mt. Everett Reservation.
Finish: Same.
Highest Point: Mt. Everett (2602 feet).
Vertical Rise: 900 feet.
Time Estimate: 2 hours.
USGS Quadrangle: Bashbish Falls.

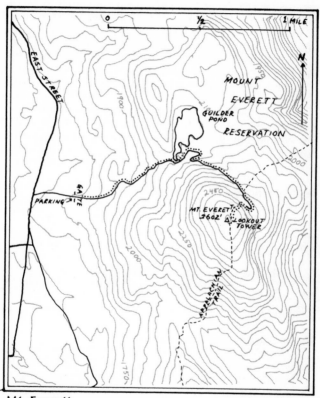

Mt. Everett

Directions to trailhead: From Great Barrington, follow Rte. 23 west towards South Egremont and Hillsdale, New York. Just past the center of South Egremont, turn left (south) onto Rte. 41. Within a few hundred yards and just after a swampy pond on the right, turn right onto Mt. Washington Rd. Follow this road along a straight stretch for about 2 mi. when suddenly the road plunges into the Taconic Range. Once the road gets into the town of Mt. Washington, there are two roads that join it from the right (west); bear left at each intersection. At the second intersection, the road becomes East St. The well-marked access road to Mt. Everett Reservation is on the left 8 mi. from the intersection of Rte. 41 and Mt. Washington Rd. Turn into the access road and park just outside of the gates which, in winter, keep motorized vehicles from using the reservation.

Trail description: This trail takes you to the top of "the Dome" of the Taconics. If, in order to get to Mt. Everett Reservation, you travel along Rte. 7 between Canaan, Connecticut, and Great Barrington, you are sure to see how Mt. Everett got its nickname. Due to its full, nearly symmetrical top, the mountain stands out from its neighbors; it is the dominant presence in the southern Berkshire landscape.

Mt. Everett Reservation is part of the Mt. Washington State Forest System. The State Forest Headquarters is located at the intersection of East and West streets, 1¼ mi. south of the entrance to the reservation. Be sure to check in at the headquarters if you are skiing alone.

From the parking area, pass the closed gates and start along the access road towards the east. The upgrade here is gentle; a good waxing job will ensure an easy climb even for inexperienced skiers. After about ¾ mi. the road passes Guilder Pond on the left. Within another few hundred yards the road switches back to the southwest near a picnic area. From here on the climb becomes a little steeper, but there are only a few short stretches where a herringbone may be required.

The road emerges from the hardwoods ½ mi. from the switchback by the picnic area. Here you begin to get an idea of the view that is in store for you once you reach the top of the mountain. Because you are now out of the shelter of the trees, this is the time to pull on a windbreaker. If you wait too long and there is a stiff breeze blowing, you will find yourself chilled through.

Shortly after the road comes out of the forest, it switches back once again, this time heading to the northwest. A small stone hut stands to the right of the trail. At the end of the straight stretch which passes the hut, turn to the southwest and follow a less distinct track which follows a twisting, steep path to the top of the mountain.

The view from the top of Mt. Everett is as fine as any other in Berkshire County. If the sun is shining and the wind is calm, you will probably want to spend some time taking it all in. If the wind is howling from the northwest, however, your stay at the summit will likely be brief. In either case, your visit to the top of the Dome is apt to be memorable.

The descent back to the parking area is exhilarating. Except for a few tricky turns at the very top, the grade is gentle enough so that only a couple of snowplows are necessary to check your speed. Because the grade is almost unbroken by level stretches, it is possible to make the entire run of 1½ mi. while having to pole or stride only once or twice. Chances are that you will find yourself wishing that the run to the parking lot went on for another 1½ mi., at least. You do not find many long, effortless descents such as this one. While it will probably take an hour to reach the top—unless you are in fine shape—the run back to the parking area will only take about 15 minutes. You may well be tempted to climb right back up so that you can enjoy the descent once again.

Bartholomew's Cobble
(Intermediate)

Territory: Bartholomew's Cobble Reservation in Ashley Falls.
Trail Length: 2 miles.
Start: Bartholomew's Cobble Parking area on Weatogue
   Road.
Finish: Same.
Highest Point: 1040 feet.
Vertical Rise: 390 feet.
Time Estimate: 1½ hours.
USGS Quadrangle: Ashley Falls.

Directions to trailhead: From Canaan, Connecticut, and
south, follow Rte. 7 north from the center of Canaan. Turn
left onto Rte. 7A at a fork 1¼ mi. north of the center of Canaan. After crossing the state border into Massachusetts,
Rte. 7A comes to a traffic light in Ashley Falls. The light
marks a 4-way intersection 1 mi. from the fork off of Rte. 7.
Turn left (southwest) at this intersection onto Andrus Rd.
Follow Andrus Rd. for 1 mi. as it crosses over the Housatonic
River. Turn left onto Weatogue Rd. about 200 yds. past the
river. Look for the Bartholomew's Cobble parking area on
the left within another couple of hundred yards.
   From Great Barrington and the north, follow Rte. 7 south
through Sheffield. Look for Rte. 7A which forks off to the
right 1¾ mi. south of the center of Sheffield. Follow Rte. 7A
for 2½ mi. until it comes to a traffic light at a 4-way intersection in the center of Ashley Falls. Turn right (southwest) at
this intersection onto Andrus Rd. and continue with the
directions above.

Trail description: Bartholomew's Cobble marks the beginning of the end of the Housatonic's lazy meander down
through the southern part of Berkshire County. North of the

144

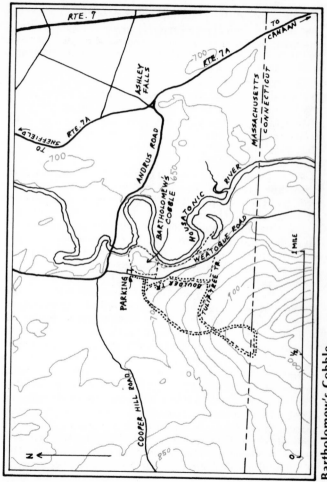

Bartholomew's Cobble

Cobble a broad flat flood plain that is pocked by swamps and oxbows stretches to Great Barrington. To the south of the area, especially over the Connecticut border, the river begins to run a straighter course, its freedom restricted by more resistant geological formations.

The Trustees of Reservations have laid out a system of trails that, for variety, equal those in any other public area in the county. Several of the trails pass an unmatched collection of fauna as they make their way towards and along the banks of the Housatonic. On the other side of Weatogue Rd., the trails are longer and straighter and therefore more suitable to skiing.

When I visited the Cobble in mid-winter, there was a chain across the entrance to the parking area. Do not let this deter you. You can park along the side of the road, as long as you make sure to pull over far enough so that one lane of traffic can get through. After you have parked, take a moment to study the map that is posted in the parking area.

Return to the entrance to the parking area and from there walk or ski south along Weatogue Rd. until you see a fence running perpendicular to the one that runs along the west side of the road. Turn right (west) onto a road that is parallel to the fence running west away from the road. Ski along the south side of the fence until you come to the northwest corner of the field. Here you will find a puzzling jumble of fences that has something to do with the sorting and (I think) loading of animals. Turn towards the southeast just after this corral and follow signs leading to the Boulder Trail, which leaves the field and heads into the woods at the southeastern corner of the field. White paint blazes mark the Boulder Trail. The trail climbs gradually for about ¼ mi. until it passes through a barbed-wire fence via a gate designed to give access to humans but not to livestock. Within another ¼ mi., the Boulder Trail comes to a T at the Tulip Tree Trail.

Turn right (west) onto the Tulip Tree Trail and ski along for a few hundred yards until you pass through another gate similar to the one on the Boulder Trail. Another ¼ mi. will take you along the northern edge of a couple of small clearings and eventually to a T at an old woods road where there is a sign reading "Summit." Turn to the left (south) and then quickly to the right (west) and enter a large field that stretches to the south and west.

Ski anywhere you like on this field, although eventually you should make your way to the top of it so that you can enjoy a nice long run back to the bottom. The very top of the field is in Connecticut while the rest of it lies in Massachusetts. To the northwest there is a fine view of Mt. Everett. When you tire of the field, leave it by the same path you entered it. But do not take a right turn and go back down the Tulip Tree Trail. Bear left instead and follow the woods road which runs downhill towards the north.

This road passes in and out of a couple of small fields and at times gets fairly steep; you may need to check your speed with a snowplow now and again. The road takes you back to the small field next to Weatogue Rd. from which you started. Because of the pitch, you will get there in no time flat and may well be tempted to climb back up the road to take advantage of the delightful downhill run one more time.

Abbey Hill
(Intermediate)

Territory: Sandisfield State Forest — West Lake Area.
Trail Length: 4½ miles.
Start: Parking area next to State Forest Headquarters on West Street.

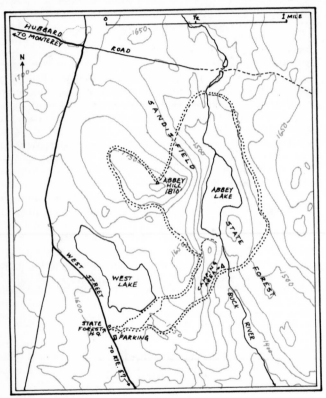

Abbey Hill

Ski-Touring Trails

Finish: Same.
Highest Point: Abbey Hill (1810 feet).
Vertical Rise: 400 feet.
Time Estimate: 2 hours.
USGS Quadrangle: Monterey.

Directions to trailhead: From Great Barrington and Rte. 7, follow Rte. 23 to the east. The junction between Rtes. 7 and 23 is about 1 mi. north of the center of Great Barrington. Follow Rte. 23 for about 8 mi. until you come to the town of Monterey. Just past the center of Monterey, turn right onto Sandisfield Rd. heading southeast. Follow Sandisfield Rd. (which becomes Hubbard Rd. when it crosses the Monterey-Sandisfield town line) for 3½ mi., until it comes to a 4-way intersection with West St. Turn right at the intersection onto West St. Follow West St. towards the south for 1¾ mi. until you see signs on the left for Sandisfield State Forest. The parking lot for the forest is about 50 yds. past the State Forest Headquarters. If the parking area has not been plowed, park behind the headquarters building.

If you find yourself in the southeastern part of the county, follow Rte. 8 to New Boston. Turn west onto Rte. 57 in New Boston and follow Rte. 57 to Sandisfield. Turn right (north) onto Pine Woods Rd. ½ mi. past the village of Sandisfield. Pine Woods Rd. (which becomes West St. after ½ mi.) is the first right-hand turn after the village. The parking area for the state forest is on the right just over 1 mi. from Rte. 57.

Trail description: For recreational use, Sandisfield State Forest is divided into two sections. Only walking, ski touring, and horseback riding are allowed in the West Lake area. In the other area south of Rte. 57, the use of snowmobiles and trail bikes is permitted. For the administrators of the state forest system in Berkshire County, this is an ideal situation; wherever they can, park planners are trying to separate skiers and snowmobilers. They probably call it something like differentiated recreational usage. Whatever they call it, they realize that, for example, skiers prefer to glide along in quiet areas on tracks of their own. You will not be bothered by snowmobiles on this trail.

The trail leads out of the parking area along an old road which heads to the east. After about 5 minutes of easy skiing, the trail turns off to the right (south) by a sign reading "Abbey Hill Foot Trail." Blue blazes mark the trail throughout. Within a couple of minutes of the first intersection, the trail crosses a small brook via a wooden bridge. A slight climb immediately after the bridge is followed by a long gradual descent, eventually leading to a campsite about ½ mi. from the bridge.

The trail passes through the campsite and within a minute or two crosses another wooden bridge. Though the waterway that passes under this bridge looks like a small creek, it is referred to on maps as the Buck River. From the banks of the mighty Buck, the trail swings to the north, rising and falling gently as it heads towards another crossing of the Buck a little over a mile from the first. Here again a small wooden bridge carries you safely over the river, which at this point measures some 3 ft. from bank to bank.

After the second crossing of the Buck, the trail swings to the southwest and ascends gently towards the top of Abbey Hill a little over ½ mi. away. The last couple of hundred yards of this climb are fairly steep; you might make easier going of it by removing your skis. From the top of Abbey Hill, follow the blue blazes as they lead off to the west. The trail descends gradually for about ½ mi. and then runs over nearly level ground for another half mile or so, until it eventually comes to a T at an old woods road. Turn right (west) here and follow the woods road for about ½ mi. until it comes to a T at a small clearing in the forest. Turn right here and follow the road as it emerges onto the flat dam that was constructed in the mid-sixties to create West Lake, lying to the right (north) of the dam.

At the end of the dam, continue along to the west through a field and towards the State Forest Headquarters visible at the top of a gentle rise.

Beartown State Forest (Intermediate)

Territory: Beartown State Forest in the towns of Great Barrington and Monterey.
Trail Length: 2-8 miles, depending on several options.
Start: Parking Area next to Benedict Pond.
Finish: Same.
Highest Point: 1850 feet.
Vertical Rise: 400 feet.
Time Estimate: 2-4 hours.
USGS Quadrangles: Great Barrington and Monterey.

Directions to trailhead: From Rte. 7 in Great Barrington, take Rte. 23 to the east for 2½ mi. until there is an intersection where smaller roads go off both to the right and the left. Turn left (north) onto Monument Valley Rd. and follow it for 1¾ mi. where you will see Blue Hill Rd. Turn right (east) onto Blue Hill Rd., the first hard-surfaced road to leave Monument Valley Rd. Follow Blue Hill Rd. for just under a mile when it comes to a T intersection. Turn right (southeast) here and continue along this extension of Blue Hill Rd., for 1½ mi. until the first left hand turn, where there is a sign for Beartown State Forest. Turn left (north) here and follow the hard road for ½ mi. to the picnic and parking area alongside Benedict Pond.

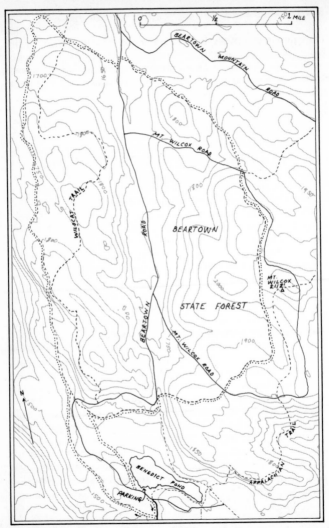

Beartown State Forest

Ski-Touring Trails

Trail description: Because I had heard that Beartown State Forest was a popular area for snowmobiling, I arrived there on a crisp Sunday in late January with some misgivings. I knew that there was a trail set aside for skiing, but I did not know if the snowmobilers would respect the rights of skiers. Happily, I neither saw nor heard any evidence of snowmobiles on the ski trail.

From the parking lot, backtrack down the access road for a couple of hundred yards and look for a trail on the right-hand side of the road marked by a red triangle. There are similar triangles at junctions along the trail, but otherwise the trail is not marked. It is kept cleared, however, and you should have no trouble finding your way.

The trail heads away from the road towards the northwest over fairly level terrain. Within ¼ mi. it swings to the north and soon parallels Beartown Rd., lying some 50 yds. away through the woods on the right (east). There is a junction in the trail after about 1 mi. Here you have a choice. If you are looking for a loop on the order of 2 mi. in length, you should cut back to the southeast here and start back for the parking area. If, on the other hand, you are looking for a longer outing that will keep you skiing for at least a couple of hours, continue on to the north.

To find your way back to the parking lot (assuming you have chosen the shorter route) turn back to the southeast at the intersection and climb a couple of hundred yards to the road. Cross the road and look for the continuation of the trail on the other side. Here the trail begins a gradual descent towards the southeast. After a few hundred yards there is a fork in the trail where you should bear right (south), and within another ½ mi. you will find yourself skiing along the shore of Benedict Pond. Keep the pond on your left, and you will soon regain the parking area. Do not ski across the pond itself. There is a spillway along this stretch where moving water keeps a small area free of ice. Even though the pond

153

may be frozen over and the ice covered with snow, there is no guarantee that the ice is safe. Remember that snow acts as insulation, and that the cold air above may not be getting through to the ice which is being warmed by the water below.

If you prefer a longer tour, keep going north at the junction mentioned above. There are several miles of fine trail ahead of you, and you can either complete the loop or turn back whenever the spirit moves you. The trail merges with a snowmobile trail about ¾ mi. north of the junction. The two trails immediately diverge once again, with the ski trail heading north and the snowmobile trail heading more to the northeast. Within a few yards of this intersection there is a small wooden shelter on the east side of the trail.

Continue along the trail towards the north for another 2 mi. when the trail begins to swing to the east. Here you will come to another intersection with the snowmobile trail. Follow the red markers as they lead you through the intersection and off to the southeast, back toward Beartown Rd. about ½ mi. away.

From this point you have two options. You can either turn around and ski back to the parking lot on the trail you have just followed, or you can follow the continuation of the ski trail on the other side of the road. Since I was tired of breaking new snow and looked forward to skiing back in the track I had just made, I chose to retrace my steps. Consequently, I have not been on that portion of the trail that makes its way up to and along the shoulder of Mt. Wilcox and then returns to Beartown Rd. Whatever route you choose, do not return to the parking area via Beartown Rd. State forest authorities are very anxious that Beartown Rd. be used by snowmobilers only. Because of the long, level straightaways, the machines are apt to get racing along at speeds that are dangerous to anyone traveling on foot. Skiers argue that they can hear the snowmobiles in time to move out of the way. And the debate continues. At any rate, why trade the tranquility of the woods for the noisy, smelly traffic along Beartown Rd.?

Pleasant Valley
(Novice)

Territory: Pleasant Valley Wildlife Sanctuary in Lenox.
Trail Length: 1½ miles.
Start: Parking area on West Mountain Road.
Finish: Same.
Highest Point: 1380 feet.
Vertical Rise: Negligible.
Time Estimate: 1 hour.
USGS Quadrangle: Pittsfield West.

Directions to trailhead: From Lenox and the south, follow Rte. 7 or 7A heading north. Look for W. Dugway Rd. and a sign for the sanctuary directly across from the Holiday Inn, ½ mi. north of the merger between 7 and 7A. Follow W. Dugway for about ¾ mi. to a 3-way intersection with W. Mountain Rd. Bear left onto W. Mountain and follow it another ¾ mi. to the sanctuary entrance.

From Pittsfield and the north, follow Rte. 7 south towards Lenox and look for the Holiday Inn on the left about 2 mi. south of Pittsfield-Lenox town line. Across from the Inn, turn right onto W. Dugway Rd. and follow directions above.

Trail description: As its name implies, the Pleasant Valley Wildlife Sanctuary is more of a nature area than a recreational area. Nevertheless, the Massachusetts Audubon Society, which owns and operates the sanctuary, welcomes

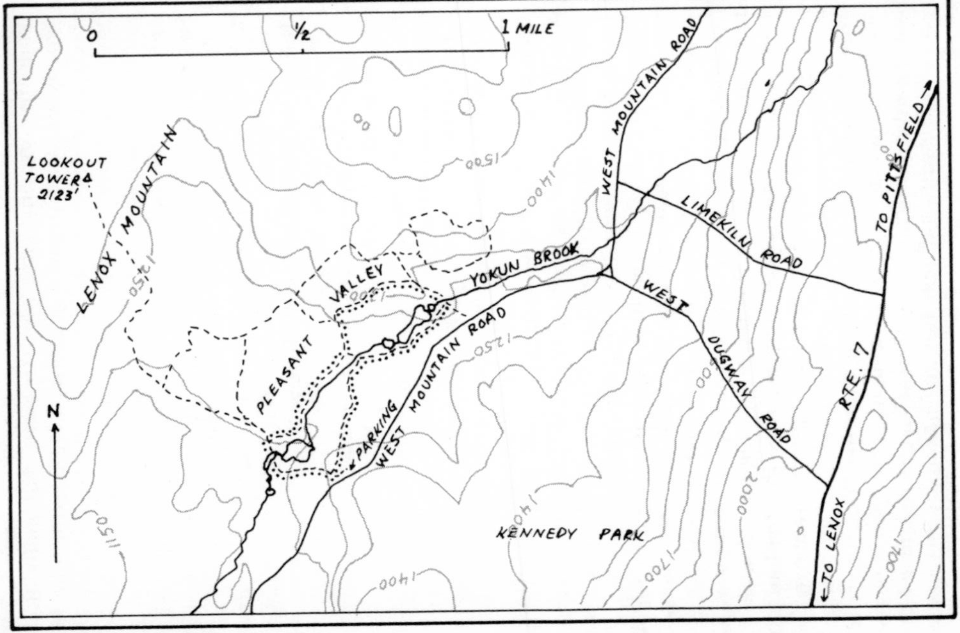

Pleasant Valley

LENOX MOUNTAIN

LOOKOUT TOWER △ 2126'

1150

PLEASANT VALLEY

1050

PARKING

WEST MOUNTAIN ROAD

1250

YOKUN BROOK

1400

1400

1350

1500

1500

KENNEDY PARK

1700

WEST MOUNTAIN ROAD

WEST DUGWAY ROAD

LIMEKILN ROAD

2000

1900

←TO LENOX

RTE. 7

TO PITTSFIELD→

1100

N

0   ½   1 MILE

Ski-Touring Trails

skiers. To defray the cost of marking and maintaining trails, there is a $2.00 charge for adults and $1.00 for residents of Lenox. For members of the Massachusetts Audubon Society there is no charge, and those under 16 years old are charged half price. The office next to the parking area is staffed every day except Monday, and a warm-up room is open to the public on weekends and holidays. A map of the trail system is available at no extra charge. You will not find any snowmobiles at Pleasant Valley, nor, due to the area's popularity among skiers, are you apt to find yourself alone. You will, on the other hand, find plenty of clean, well-tended trails and a friendly, helpful staff.

Marked ski trails are limited to those which run over near-ly level ground on either side of Yokun Brook. You can also use several other trails which lead away from the brook towards Lenox Mountain, but these are not marked for skiers. For walking during the warmer months, all the trails in the sanctuary are blazed with one of three colors: blue blazes mark trails which head away from the parking lot, yellow blazes mark trails returning to the parking lot, and white blazes mark cross trails. With this marking system in mind, do not hesitate to explore some of the more remote trails if the spirit moves you.

The loop used most frequently by skiers heads west away from the entrance gate and is called the Nature Trail. Follow this trail for about ¼ mi. when it crosses over Pike's Pond via a wooden footbridge. On the other (north) side of the bridge, the Nature Trail swings to the east and intersects with another trail within a couple of hundred yards. Bear left (east) here onto the Yokun Trail. Stay on this trail for a little under ½ mi. as it passes four other side trails. At the fifth intersection it comes to a T with the Old Wood Rd. Turn right (east) onto the Old Wood Rd. and follow it for about ¼ mi. past two other side trails until it crosses over Yokun Brook on another wooden footbridge. Turn right (west) once you are over the bridge and start back towards the parking area.

At an intersection about ¼ mi. from the last bridge, you will see a large clearing to your left (south). Turn up into this field and climb back up to the parking area.

There are so many trails and intersections in the sanctuary that you might have trouble following the directions above. Remember that the area is relatively small and that you cannot get lost for long. In the event that you do get a bit disoriented, look for the yellow blazes that lead back to the parking lot.

Woods Pond
(Novice)

Territory: Along the banks of the Housatonic River in Lee and Lenox.
Trail Length: 5 miles.
Start: Parking area on Woodland Street in Lee.
Finish: Same.
Highest Point: 1010 feet.
Vertical Rise: Negligible.
Time Estimate: 1½-2 hours.
USGS Quadrangles: East Lee and Pittsfield East.

Directions to trailhead: From Pittsfield and the north, Rte. 7 south towards Lenox. Bear left on Rte. 7 at the fork between Rtes. 7 and 7A just north of Lenox. Turn left onto Housatonic St. 1¼ mi. south of the fork.

From the southern part of the county, follow either Rte. 20 or Rte. 7 north towards Pittsfield. Turn right onto Housatonic St. 1 mi. north of the point where Rtes. 20 and 7 merge just

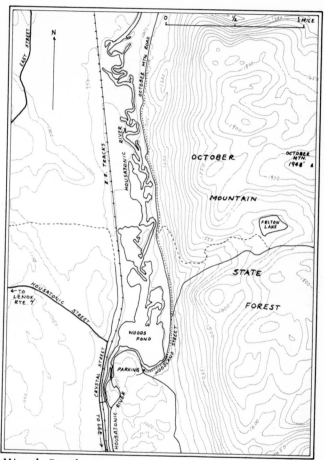

Woods Pond

south of Lenox.

From the center of Lenox, take Housatonic St. to the east towards and across Rte. 7.

Once you are on Housatonic St., follow it east from Rte. 7 for 1¼ mi. until it comes to the bottom of a long hill. Turn right (south) onto Crystal St. which parallels an old set of railroad tracks and the Housatonic River, both of which are on the left of the road. Go south on Crystal St. for a little less than ½ mi. and take the first turn to the left. This turn is not marked but is recognizable since it is the first left turn off of Crystal and it is just before a long string of abandoned warehouses on the left, across the railroad tracks. The road immediately crosses the tracks and within 50 yds. crosses the river on a green steel bridge. On the far side of the bridge, turn to the left (north). The road crosses another bridge within a couple of hundred yards of the first. Turn to the left after crossing this bridge. The road now heads to the north, but it soon swings to the east and then to the southeast as it parallels the shore of Woods Pond on the left. Continue along this road for about ¾ mi. until it leaves the shores of the pond. Just as it does so, there is an unplowed road leading off to the left (southeast). A small plowed area on the left serves as a parking lot.

Trail description: This trail takes you along the southern shore of Woods Pond before it swings to the north and runs along the eastern edge of the pond and then the eastern bank of the Housatonic River for 2½ mi. The trail is nearly level throughout and is therefore suited to the novice as well as the more experienced skier. Because of its proximity to October Mountain State Forest and that area's popularity with snowmobilers, at times there can be a substantial amount of noisy traffic along the first mile of the trail, but usually only on weekends. If you can manage to ski this trail on a weekday—especially on a bright afternoon when the sun in the west lights up the pond and the river—you will probably avoid any meetings with snowmobilers.

The road—called Woodland St. while it is in Lenox and October Mtn. or Woods Pond Rd. once it crosses the Lee-Lenox town line about halfway up the trail—is joined from both sides by several other dirt roads and smaller trails. At every intersection, go straight ahead. Except for a few minor wiggles, the road heads just about due north all the way to the end of that section of it which can be skied. Eventually, 2½ mi. north of the parking area, the unplowed section of the road ends. It is kept open from the northern end for people living in a few houses along October Mtn. Rd. When you come to the end of the unplowed section, simply turn around and ski back over the route you just followed. Avoid, if possible, the temptation to take one of the side trails which leads east into October Mountain State Forest. State forest officials are trying to discourage skiing in the forest because of the volume of snowmobile traffic and because there are no trails which are reserved specifically for skiing. Skiers will welcome the day when they are encouraged to use this state forest, which is not only located very near the center of the county but is also the largest state forest within the county.

Kennedy Park
(Intermediate)

Territory: John D. Kennedy Park in the town of Lenox.
Trail Length: 3-4 miles.
Start: Parking lot on west side of Main Street (Route 7A). Also parking lot behind Lenox House Restaurant on Route 7.
Finish: Same.

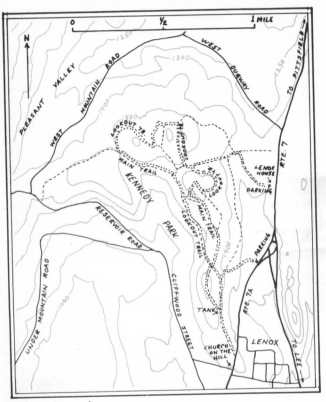

Kennedy Park

Ski-Touring Trails

Highest Point: Approximately 1550 feet.
Vertical Rise: 300-400 feet.
Time Estimate: 1½ hours.
USGS Quadrangles: Stockbridge and Pittsfield West.

Directions to trailhead: There are several entrances to Kennedy Park. You can get to the park on foot from the center of Lenox by walking north on Main St. to the Church on the Hill. In back of the church there is an unpaved road leading north-northwest into the park.

If you are coming by car, park either at the Kennedy Park parking area or behind the Lenox House. To get to the former from the center of Lenox, follow Rte. 7 (Main St.) north up the hill past the Church on the Hill on the left and drive almost to the interchange with Rtes. 7 and 20. Fifty yds. before an island that separates traffic for the interchange, look for a small parking lot on the left. A wooden fence borders the parking lot and there is a sign which is not easily legible from a moving car. From Pittsfield and the north, follow Rte. 7 south until the fork just north of Lenox. Here, bear right onto Rte. 7A and look for the parking lot on the right immediately after the traffic island.

If you choose to park at the Lenox House, you will find the restaurant on the west side of Rte. 7 about ½ mi. north of the interchange mentioned above.

Trail description: The John D. Kennedy Park lies on the property of the old Aspinwall Hotel, built in 1902 to accommodate the wealthy who wanted to spend time in Lenox hobnobbing with their elite colleagues who had built summer "cottages" in the area. The hotel burned down in 1931, and the property was taken over by the town in 1957 and transformed into a park. The trails in the park are well marked, well maintained, and reserved for foot traffic only.

If you came into the park via the dirt road behind the

163

Church on the Hill, follow the Main Trail (marked by white triangular blazes.) At first the trail heads almost due north, but it soon swings to the northwest and intersects with the Lookout Trail just under 1 mi. from the church. There are several trails which merge and diverge along the way. You will know the main trail by its width and by the white blazes. When you get to the intersection with the Lookout Trail, turn right (north) onto the Lookout Trail which is marked by red diamond-shaped blazes. The Lookout Trail snakes its way to the north, east, north again, west, and finally south before it rejoins the Main Trail. There are several intersections along this loop, but you will not make a wrong turn if you follow the red blazes. There are also some fairly steep pitches both up and down, but they are short and should pose no problem for an intermediate skier. Remember that the park is very popular with cross-country skiers and you are not apt to be alone, especially on the weekends.

When the Lookout Trail finally rejoins the Main Trail, turn left (east) onto the Main Trail and follow the white triangles back to the church. If you have the time and energy, do not hesitate to explore any of the several side trails you come upon. You cannot really get lost in Kennedy Park; within a few minutes on any trail you are bound to meet up with either the Main or Lookout Trails.

If you park in the Kennedy Park parking area alongside Rte. 7A, look for the Lookout Trail (red diamond blazes) which leaves the western border of the parking area. There is a bit of steep climbing here and in places the trail is narrow; you might be better off walking up this first leg of the trail. Within a couple of hundred yards, the trail comes out on an old woods road. Follow the red blazes as they jog to the left and then back to the right joining the Main Trail. Ski along the Main Trail (white triangular blazes) for ½ mi. until the Lookout Trail turns off to the right (north). Follow the red blazes of the Lookout Trail as it twists and turns its way for

Ski-Touring Trails

1¼ mi. past several intersections (always follow the red blazes) through nearly every point of the compass.

Eventually the Lookout Trail comes out onto the Main Trail again. Follow the white blazes of the Main Trail back to the point where the two trails intersect once again just above the parking area. From here, follow the red diamonds back down the hill to the parking area.

From the parking lot behind the Lenox House, follow a trail that leads northwest across a clearing and into the woods. Just after the trail enters the woods there is a 4-way intersection; turn left (west) here and ski straight ahead past two other intersections and up a steady but gentle grade for about ¼ mi. until the trail intersects with the Lookout Trail. Take a minute to make a mental picture of this intersection; you are going to have to make a turn here on the way out of the park. Bear (right) west at the intersection and follow the red blazes of the Lookout Trail for about a mile through several intersections to the Main Trail. Turn left (east) onto the Main Trail (white blazes) and ski for 1 mi. past several side trails until the Main Trail intersects with the Lookout Trail for the second time. Here, double back to the north onto the Lookout Trail. The Lookout Trail runs through a fairly steep and narrow stretch here. Stick with the Lookout Trail which crosses the Main Trail (to make matters even more confusing) and, after another ¼ mi., returns to the intersection you made a mental note of and where you first turned onto the Lookout Trail. Turn right (east) here and enjoy a fine downhill run for ¼ mi. to the 4-way intersection near the parking area behind the Lenox House. Turn right (south) here and follow the trail out of the woods to the parking area.

Due to the many intersections and side trails, it is a bit tricky finding your way over a prescribed route if you are skiing in Kennedy Park for the first time. The accompanying map should help. Also, remember that you are never more than 1 mi. from the nearest entrance to the area.

Canoe Meadows
(Novice)

Territory: Massachusetts Audubon Society Sanctuary at Canoe Meadows in Pittsfield.
Trail Length: 1½-2 miles.
Start: Parking area off of Holmes Road.
Finish: Same.
Highest Point: 1040 feet.
Vertical Rise: Negligible.
Time Estimate: 30 minutes or as long as you like.
USGS Quadrangle: Pittsfield East.

Directions to trailhead: From Park Square in the center of Pittsfield, follow East St. towards the east for about six blocks. Turn left (south) onto Elm St. which crosses the East Branch of the Housatonic River within a couple of hundred yards and then angles towards the east. Turn right (south) onto Holmes Rd., ½ mi. after Elm St. crosses the river. The entrance to Canoe Meadows is on the left (east) side of Holmes Rd. just under 1 mi. from Elm St. If you cross the river on Holmes Rd., you have gone too far. Turn around and look for the entrance on the right about 100 yds. north of the river.

From Lenox and the south, follow Rte. 7 north towards Pittsfield. Turn right (east) onto Holmes Rd. at a traffic light which is just over 3 mi. north of Lenox. Stay on Holmes Rd. for a little over 3½ mi. Look for the entrance to Canoe Meadows on the right about 100 yds. past the bridge over the Housatonic River.

Trail description: This area is perfectly suited to the novice skier or the more experienced skier who wants some easy open terrain to practice on. The trail is not very long and there is little climbing to be done. Because of its convenient

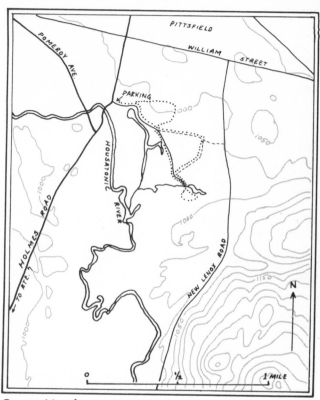

Canoe Meadows

location, Canoe Meadows is a popular spot on weekends when the Massachusetts Audubon Society employs an attendant to answer questions, provide maps, and collect a $1.00 fee which goes toward maintenance of the area. The society is a non-profit organization.

From the parking lot, ski down a very gentle grade towards the east. Once it levels out, the trail swings to the south within a couple of hundred yards and then quickly back to the east. Here there is a fork in the road, just past a small building on the left. Bear left (east) at the fork and follow this trail into the woods. After ¼ mi. on this leg, turn right (south) onto another trail which heads first to the south and then to the southwest. Turn left (southeast) after another ¼ mi. when the trail comes to a T at the road you started on.

This trail crosses Sackett Brook within a couple of hundred yards and leaves you in a field next to a small pond and just about at the far end of the Canoe Meadows property. After a swing around this field, head back across Sackett Brook and follow the road to the parking lot without making any turns.

You should be able to find plenty of elbow room in the large fields near the parking area if you are looking for some space to learn how to get around on skis to begin with, or if you are perfecting your stride for a race or a major excursion into the back country.

Honwee-Turner Loop
(Intermediate)

Territory: Pittsfield State Forest.
Trail Length: 4½ miles.
Start: Parking area at the end of Cascade Street.

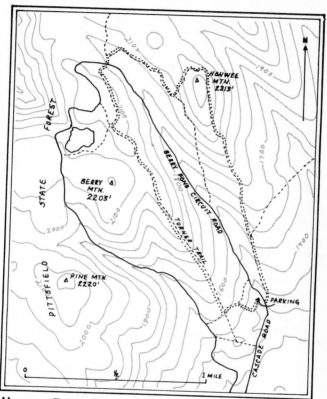

Honwee-Turner Loop

Finish: Same.
Highest Point: Honwee Mountain (2313 feet).
Vertical Rise: 1040 feet.
Time Estimate: 2 hours.
USGS Quadrangles: Hancock and Pittsfield West.

Directions to trailhead: From the center of Pittsfield, follow West St. to the west for 2½ mi. Turn right (north) onto Churchill St. Follow Churchill for 1¾ mi. Turn left at a sign for Pittsfield State Forest. After another ½ mi., turn right onto Cascade St. and enter the state forest within ½ mi. Pass the entrance gate and go straight ahead for a little over ½ mi. where the road angles to the left (northwest). Within a couple of hundred yards of this turn is a parking lot on the left directly across from a small brown cabin. Park here.

Trail description: Honwee Mtn. is the tallest of several Taconic summits within Pittsfield State Forest. While the top of the mountain is relatively flat and overgrown with hardwoods, in the winter it is possible to get a view of the surrounding countryside through the trees. There is quite a bit of climbing to do on this trail and the descent down the Turner Trail is steep; make sure your climbing and stopping skills are in good working order before tackling this trail.

The trail starts across the road from the parking area about 20 yds. to the right (southeast) of the brown cabin. It is marked initially by an orange triangle, the symbol used in this and other state forests to denote snowmobile trails. Efforts are being made to segregate skiers and snowmobilers in Pittsfield State Forest, but as yet the boundaries are unresolved. To make sure about them, check in with the superintendent at the State Forest Headquarters near the entrance gate. While I saw some snowmobile tracks on the first leg of this trail, traffic is reportedly light, especially on weekdays.

Ski-Touring Trails

Within a few yards of the road, the trail forks. Bear left here and begin to follow a trail that is marked by white blazes painted onto the trees.

The trail forks again after about ½ mi. To the left is a trail that heads for Balance Rock. Bear left at this fork and continue to climb towards the north-northwest and the summit of Honwee about 1 mi. away. For the most part the grade from the last fork to the top of the mountain is gentle, although there is one stretch after the halfway point that is fairly steep. Even if your skis are properly waxed, you will probably have to shift into a herringbone or side-step approach through this section. The steep part of the climb does not last more than a couple of hundred yards, however, and eventually the trail levels out completely as it passes over the broad, flat summit of Honwee Mtn. You may not even realize that you are on the top until you start to go downhill again.

The trail leaves the top of the mountain heading almost due north, but soon swings to the west as it runs downhill through a steep stretch for 200-300 yds.; you will need to use a snowplow to check your speed and maintain control. At the bottom of this stretch is a junction with another trail which leads off to the north. Bear left (southwest) at this intersection and follow a winding trail downhill (past another side trail that goes off to the right) and for another ¼ mi. until the trail comes to a T. This last section is marked by white rectangular blazes, but not as frequently as was the segment of the trail between the parking lot and the top of Honwee.

Turn to the right (northwest) at the T and ski along this unmarked trail for about ¼ mi. until it comes to another T about 20 yds. uphill from a small creek on the left (west). Turn left at this intersection, cross the brook, and climb up about 30 yds. to Berry Pond Circuit Rd., which is paved but not plowed in the winter.

Go directly across the road and start towards the west on

another trail, this one marked now and again by the orange triangles. This section of the trail climbs first to the southwest and then to the southeast as it makes its way towards a stand of evergreens about ½ mi. from the road.

The trail goes through the evergreens and comes to a 4-way intersection a few hundred yards beyond them. Turn left (east) at this intersection which is marked by a single orange triangle, and begin to ski down the Turner Trail heading generally towards the southeast. After about 1¼ mi. of a steady, sometimes fairly steep descent, the Turner Trail comes to a 4-way intersection. Turn to the left (east) here and ski a couple of hundred yards until the trail you are now on emerges from the woods onto an open slope sometimes used for downhill skiing.

Turn to the right and ski down the slope bearing left towards the bottom; as the slope ends so does this trail. The parking lot is on the far side of Lulu Brook which borders the bottom of the open slope. A wooden bridge spans the small stream.

Notchview
(Intermediate)

Territory: Notchview Reservation in the town of Windsor.
Trail Length: 5 miles.
Start: Parking lot next to Budd Visitor Center.
Finish: Same.
Highest Point: Judges Hill (2297 feet).
Vertical Rise: 450 feet.
Time Estimate: 2½ hours.
USGS Quadrangle: Windsor.

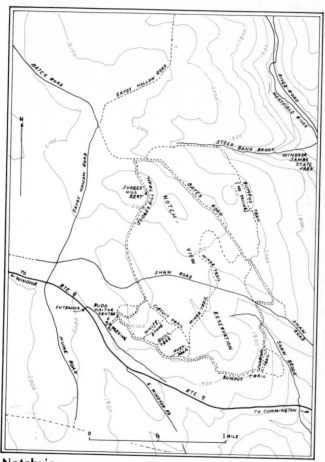

Notchview

Directions to trailhead: From Pittsfield and the west, take Rte. 9 (also Rte. 8A once you pass through Dalton) heading east towards Windsor and Northampton. When 8A turns off to the left (north) at Windsor, check the odometer in your car. The sign marking the entrance to Notchview Reservation is on the left exactly 1 mi. after the intersection of Rtes. 9 and 8A.

From Northampton and the east, follow Rte. 9 towards Windsor and Pittsfield. The turnoff for Notchview Reservation is on the right (north) side of the road 3½ mi. past the Cummington-Windsor town line, also the boundary between Berkshire and Hampshire counties. If you find yourself at the intersection of Rtes. 9 and 8A, you have gone too far. Reverse your direction at the intersection and measure 1 mi. on your odometer. Going east now, the entrance to Notchview will be on the left side of Rte. 9.

Trail description: Since the area is very popular with cross-country skiers, several of the trails in Notchview are apt to have established tracks, except, of course, immediately after a heavy snowfall. In general, the trails are very well marked and maintained. There is an admission charge of $ .50 for use of the area, and for another $ .20 a fine map can be purchased. On weekends and holidays, the Budd Visitor Center is open offering warmth and a place to wax your skis. While snowmobiles are not allowed on the reservation, they can pass through it on either Shaw or Bates roads. Use of these roads by snowmobilers is reported to be light.

From the parking area, ski north past a sign reading "Trail" and enter the woods. Turn right (east) within a few yards at an intersection with the Circuit Trail. Your climbing skills will be tested right away as the trail goes up a short, steep rise. From the top of the rise the trail—marked by yellow blazes—descends gradually to the southeast. Within a few minutes the trail passes by the Whitestone, the Quill Tree, and the Mushroom trails on the left and a large shed on the right. Do not turn off onto any of these side trails. Go straight ahead on the Bumpus Trail which emerges into a large field within a few hundred yards of the shed.

Follow a series of yellow-topped fence posts which mark the trail as it heads to the east passing an old cellar hole and barn on the right. The trail leaves the field at the far right (southeastern) corner. Once you are in the middle of the field you may want to ski directly across the field instead of following the fence posts around the perimeter. Though the downgrade is gradual, you may get going fairly quickly across the field. Check your speed before entering the woods.

Follow the Bumpus Trail for ¼ mi. through the woods until you see a sign marking the Charcoal Trail on the left. Turn left (north) onto the Charcoal Trail which rejoins the Bumpus Trail within a few hundred yards. The trail can be difficult through this stretch as it is quite narrow, and there are several twists and turns on the way down to a wooden footbridge which crosses Shaw Brook. Once over the bridge the trail climbs a fairly steep grade for a couple of hundred yards until it comes out onto Shaw Rd. Cross the road and pick up the trail again on the other side. The trail heads east away from the road and up a gentle rise until it emerges into another large clearing; the trail is now heading north. Once again you should look for the yellow-blazed fence posts which lead you across the clearing in a northwesterly direction. If the sun is shining and the wind is nearly calm, this is probably the spot for a picnic if you are carrying one. Even if there is a little breeze, you should be able to find shelter somewhere along the edge of the woods.

When the trail comes to the northern boundary of the field, turn left (west), ski past a few trees, and turn right onto Bates Rd. Here you get a fine opportunity to practice your stride as the road is nearly level and the turns are very gentle. Follow Bates Rd. to the northwest for about a mile and then turn left (south) onto Judges Hill Trail at a well-marked intersection.

Here you are faced with a steep climb that will almost surely leave you out of breath by the time you reach the top of Judges Hill. The descent down the south side of the hill is not as steep, but there are some sharp turns and you should take it slowly. Eventually the trail levels off and you can get back to a comfortable pace for about ½ mi. until the trail comes out onto Shaw Rd. once again. Cross the road and pick up the trail on the other side. Within a couple of hundred level yards of the road, the trail comes to an intersection where there is a sign directing you towards the Visitor Center about ¼ mi. away.

North Pond
(Intermediate)

Territory: Savoy Mountain State Forest.
Trail Length: 2½ miles.
Start: Parking area at the North Pond Recreation Area.
Finish: Same.
Highest Point: 2240 feet.
Vertical Rise: 320 feet.
Time Estimate: 1 hour.
USGS Quadrangle: North Adams.

Directions to trailhead: From Adams, take Rte. 116 east towards Savoy. After 7 mi., Rte. 116 is joined by Rte. 8A which comes into Rte. 116 from the right (south). Stay on 116 for another ½ mi., and then turn left (north) onto Center Rd.

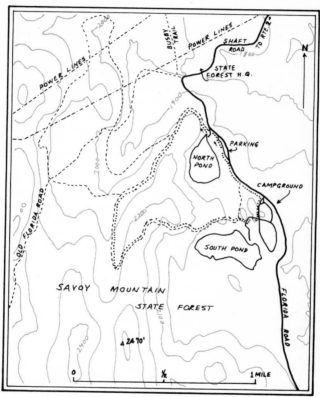

North Pond

which is not well marked. If you miss Center Rd., stay on Rte. 116 for another few hundred yards and stop and ask directions at the Savoy general store on the right side of the road. Once you are on Center Rd., follow it for 3 mi. until it comes to a T intersection with Adams Rd. Turn left (west) onto Adams Rd., the only possible direction since the road is not plowed to the right (east) of this intersection. Within a few hundred yards turn right (north) off of Adams Rd. onto New State Rd. Follow New State for 1¾ mi. until it comes to another T. Turn left (west) here — again the left turn is your only choice — and follow this road past a large parking lot on the right which is used by snowmobilers. Follow the road to the west and then to the north for 2¼ mi. Here there is a parking lot on the left (west) side of the road. If you find yourself driving past a fenced-in building with a couple of garage doors on the side facing the road, you have gone too far. This is the State Forest Headquarters building. Turn around and drive back about ½ mi. and look for the entrance to the parking area on the right side of the road.

From North Adams, follow Rte. 2 east until you come to the West Summit where there are a couple of tourist shops and an observation tower. Follow Rte. 2 to the east for ½ mi. to Shaft Rd. which turns off to the right (south). Stay to the right at the first intersection about ½ mi. down Shaft Rd. At the second intersection, 1 mi. after the first, go straight ahead. (On your left at this intersection is a fenced-in building with a couple of strange looking cones projecting out of one side. This is the central shaft for the Hoosac Tunnel which carries rail traffic beneath the Hoosac Range. When the tunnel was being built between 1851 and 1875, men were lowered down this shaft to dig from the center of the tunnel out to both ends. Today the shaft is used to ventilate the tunnel.) Continue along Shaft Rd. for about ½ mi. where the road forks. Bear right here and look for the parking area on the right about 1 mi. further along Shaft Rd.

Ski-Touring Trails

Trail description: To date, trails for cross-country skiing in Savoy Mountain State Forest are somewhat limited, considering the tremendous size of the forest. This is unfortunate since it is a lovely area, and, because of the elevation, the snows come early in the year and linger on well after the ground is bare in lower and more southern parts of the county. While an effort is being made to expand the ski trails in the forest, it is obvious that snowmobilers have the best of this area in terms of the length and variety of trails reserved for their use. The personnel at the State Forest Headquarters are conscientious and sensitive to the needs of skiers; they should be encouraged in their efforts to develop and map present and future ski trails.

From the parking area walk or ski north along the road for about 200 yds. until you see an unplowed road on the left. The trail, which is marked by blue triangles, starts on the right (northern) side of this road right beside a gate. For the first few hundred yards the trail parallels Shaft Rd. but it then swings away from the road towards the southwest. After about ½ mi. the trail comes to a 3-way intersection. Straight ahead is the beginning of another loop designed for skiing, but it is not all that well marked according to the staff at State Forest Headquarters. Since I have not skied this particular loop, I cannot vouch for it one way or the other, but you might take a crack at it if you feel like exploring.

The main trail leaves the intersection heading due south. It then climbs gently towards the southwest, then to the south again, and finally descends to the east. Eventually it comes to another 3-way intersection about 1½ mi. after the first. Turn right (east) here and ski over a small rise into the North Pond camping area. Here the trail merges with the clear tracks of a touring course used by the Williams College cross-country ski team. Turn left and parallel this course as it climbs a slight rise towards a clearing to the east. Once you get into the clearing, turn left (north) and ski along the western edge of the campground until it meets Shaft Rd. Turn to the left on the road and follow it for about ¼ mi. back to the parking area.

Historic Valley Park
(Intermediate)

Territory: Historic Valley Park in North Adams.
Trail Length: 1½-2 miles.
Start: Parking area next to Windsor Lake.
Finish: Same.
Highest Point: 870 feet.
Vertical Rise: 100 feet.
Time Estimate: 30 minutes or as long as you like.
USGS Quadrangle: North Adams.

Directions to trailhead: Drive east on Main St. in North Adams past the downtown area to the intersection of East Main and Church streets. Turn right (south) onto Church St. Follow Church St. towards the southeast for ¾ mi. Turn left into Bradley St. which goes up a fairly steep grade for ¼ mi. and ends. Turn right at the end of Bradley St. onto the access road for Historic Valley Park. The parking area is on the left about 150 yds. past the entrance.

Trail description: The cross-country skiing craze has caught on to such a degree that even city parks are now including trails within their bounds. When there is some open land within the city limits, why should skiers have to drive several miles to ski? Historic Valley Park is not a typical urban park, to be sure, but it does lie within the limits of the city of North

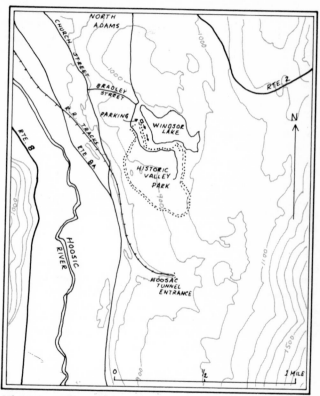

Historic Valley Park

Adams.

The trail through the park is lacking in length, but it gets more use than many of the other trails described in this book simply because it is so accessible. Residents of North Adams are able to get in a little skiing after work or even during lunch hour.

From the parking area, ski along the road past a gate and around the southwestern edge of Windsor Lake until you come to a brown garage on the right side of the road. Turn to the left just past this building and pick up the trail which starts next to another building on the shore of the lake about 100 yds. away from the garage.

From here the trail heads off to the south. The trail is well marked by signs which describe the relative difficulty of each section. There are a couple of sharp drops and climbs, but they are extremely short and need cause no apprehension even for beginners. The trail eventually swings to the west as it passes through the forest and then crosses a small brook on a wooden footbridge. Shortly after the bridge the trail turns back to the north and within ¼ mi. it emerges from the woods onto the access road. Turn left here and ski a couple of hundred yards to the parking area. Or, if you are just getting warmed up, turn right on the road and take another turn around the circuit.

Do not ski on the lake unless you are certain that the ice is sufficiently thick. Along the southwest side of the lake there is a spillway where there is apt to be some open water even when the temperature is well below freezing.

Rockwell Road
(Intermediate)

Territory: Mt. Greylock State Reservation.

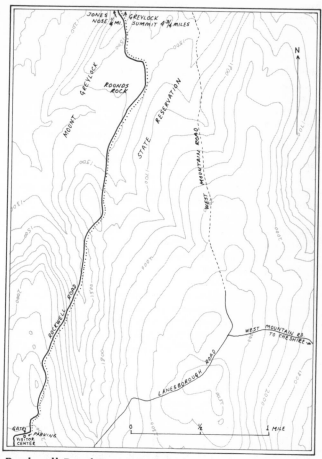

Rockwell Road Part I (South)

Trail Length: 8 miles (to Jones Nose and return), 15 miles (to Stony Ledge and return), or 17 miles (to Mt. Greylock summit and return).

Start: Parking area at Mt. Greylock Visitor Center.

Finish: Same.

Highest Point: 2440 feet (Jones Nose), 2580 feet (Stony Ledge), or 3487 feet (Mt. Greylock summit).

Vertical Rise: 660 feet (Jones Nose), 800 feet (Stony Ledge), or 1710 feet (Greylock).

Time Estimate: 3-6 hours.

USGS Quadrangles: Cheshire and Williamstown.

Directions to trailhead: From Pittsfield and the south, follow Rte. 7 north towards Lanesborough and Williamstown. Turn right off Rte. 7 onto North Main St. 1½ mi. north of the center of Lanesborough. Follow North Main for ¾ mi. until it comes to a 3-way intersection. Turn right (east) here onto Quarry Rd. Bear left onto Rockwell Rd. at a fork ½ mi. up Quarry Rd. The Visitor Center for Mt. Greylock Reservation is on the right ½ mi. from the beginning of Rockwell Rd. The parking area is on the far (east) side of the Visitor Center.

From Williamstown and the north, follow Rte. 7 south towards Lanesborough and Pittsfield. Turn left (east) onto North Main St. just over 4 mi. south of the New Ashford-Lanesborough town line. If you miss the turn and find yourself in the center of Lanesborough, turn around and go 1½ mi. north along Rte. 7 and look for North Main on the right side of the highway.

Trail description: Rockwell Rd. heads north from the Visitor Center and, 8½ mi. later, ends at the summit of Mt. Greylock, the highest point in Massachusetts. One mi. short of the summit, it intersects with the southern end of Notch Rd. which provides access to the reservation from Rte. 2 in North Adams. Both roads are wide enough to allow 2-way

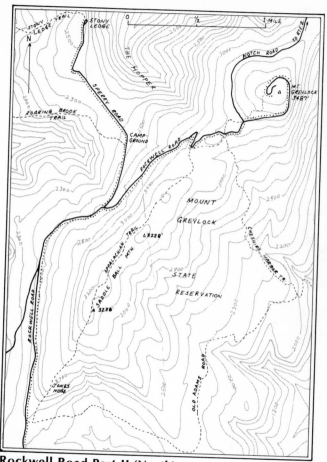

Rockwell Road Part II (North)

automobile traffic in the warmer months. The roads are not plowed in the winter.

The trip to either Stony Ledge or to the summit of Mt. Greylock will take several hours, and you should plan to carry some food and drink and an extra layer of clothing. Even though the temperature may be relatively mild at the Visitor Center, you can count on it being much cooler and probably windier at either of the exposed destinations. Remember also that the notoriously fickle weather in this area can transform what may start as a lovely tour into a dangerous outing in a matter of hours. Keep an eye on the weather as you make your way towards the north.

Mt. Greylock Reservation is a popular area for snowmobiling and you can be sure of plenty of noisy traffic on the weekends. If the presence of the machines ruins a day of skiing for you, make sure to ski this trail during the middle of the week when the mountain is relatively free of snowmobiles.

From the parking area, ski through the heavy iron gates that block off Rockwell Rd. just after it passes the Visitor Center. For the first ½ mi. or so, the road is fairly steep but never steep enough so that a good waxing job cannot handle it. After this initial rise the road levels out, although there are gentle climbs and dips throughout. In the 4 mi. between the Visitor Center and Jones Nose, the road only climbs some 600 ft. This hardly qualifies as an arduous ascent. As the road approaches Jones Nose and the intersection with the Appalachian Trail and Old Adams Rd., there is a noticeable thinning of the forest on either side. Now and again there is an opening large enough to be mistaken for a trail. The clearing by Jones Nose that serves as a parking area in the summertime is on the right side of the road. If the snow is not too deep you will be able to identify the clearing by a heavy wooden barricade that blocks a gap in the trees on the north side of the clearing. The barricade is meant to keep any vehicles off of the Appalachian Trail, which heads north from the clearing, parallels the somewhat indistinct ridge line of Saddle Ball Mtn., and eventually passes over the summit of Mt. Greylock on its way north to Vermont and on into Maine. Although the trail is too narrow and, in places, too steep to ski, the first few hundred yards on the way up Jones Nose are negotiable. Do not hesitate to climb up a ways so that you can enjoy the fine view of the surrounding countryside. If the weather is reasonably mild, this is a good spot for a picnic, although there is little shelter from the wind.

If, once you reach Jones Nose, you find blisters beginning to form and muscles beginning to ache, you should retire gracefully and head back down Rockwell Rd. to the parking area. If, on the other hand, you find everything holding up reasonably well and you are anxious to extend the tour, continue along the road to the north.

After about 1 mi. you will pass Ash Fort, a stone monument on the left (west) side of the trail. Another mile will bring you to the intersection of Rockwell and Sperry roads. The latter road forks to the left and passes through a campground within ½ mi. From the campground, Sperry Rd. continues along to the northwest for another mile until it ends at Stony Ledge; here there is a beautiful view of the Hopper, a glacial cirque which lies between Stony Ledge and the main body of the mountain to the east.

If reaching the summit is your goal, go right at the fork with Sperry Rd. and continue along Rockwell Rd. towards the northeast. One and one-half mi. from the fork, Rockwell comes to a 3-way intersection. To the left (northwest) is Notch Rd. Bear right at the intersection and follow Rockwell which leads to the top of the mountain, just under a mile away. This last stretch is a bit steep, but think what fun you will have gliding back down it after your visit to the summit.

The view from the top of Greylock is spectacular. To the east lies the Hoosac River Valley with the Hoosac Range beyond. The Green Mountains and much of southern Vermont are visible to the north, and to the west are the Taconics and the Catskills in New York State beyond them.

When you have finished taking in the sights, start back down by the same route you followed on the way up. The return trip will take a little less time since there is less climbing to do, but, as you are sure to have noticed on the way up, there is plenty of level ground to be covered. Unfortunately it is not one continuous 8½ mi. descent. Each time you begin to despair at the length of the trip, however, you seem to come to a downhill stretch where you can glide along peacefully and catch your breath.

Berlin Mountain
(Intermediate)

Territory: Taconic Range in Williamstown along New York-Massachusetts border.
Trail Length: 4½ miles.
Start: Parking area at Williams College Ski Area.
Finish: Same.
Highest Point: Berlin Mountain (2798 feet).
Vertical Rise: 1300 feet.
Time Estimate: 2 hours.
USGS Quadrangle: Berlin, New York.

Directions to trailhead: From the intersection of Rtes. 2 and 7, which is 2¼ mi. south of the center of Williamstown, turn onto Rte. 2 heading west towards Taconic Trail State Park and Petersburg, New York. As Rte. 2 begins immediately to climb to the west, look for a small road off to the left just

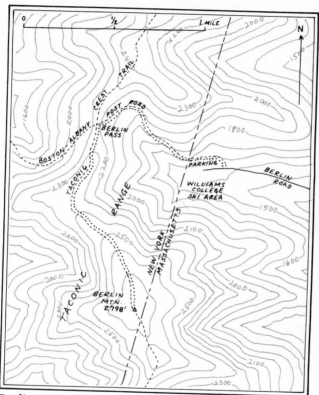

Berlin Mountain

over ¼ mi. from the intersection of Rtes. 2 and 7. Turn left here onto Torrey Woods Rd. which is also marked by a sign reading "Carmelite Novitiate." Within ½ mi. of the beginning of Torrey Woods Rd., there is a 3-way intersection. Oblong Rd. runs off to the left (south) from this intersection. Go straight ahead onto what is now called Berlin Rd. Bear left at a fork ¾ mi. up Berlin and continue on to the parking area at the end of the road, another 1¼ mi. to the west.

Trail description: As you can see from the vertical rise (1300 ft.), there is a good deal of climbing to be done on this tour. Before you turn your back on this trail, however, remember that the spectacular view from the top of Berlin Mtn. and the long run back down to the parking area make the exertion worthwhile. Make sure that your snowplow is in good working order before you tackle this trail.

The trail leaves the parking area on the northern edge of the clearing. Right away there is a short steep stretch, but the pitch decreases within about 50 yds. as the trail swings to the west. From here on up to Berlin pass—a distance of 1 mi.—the trail climbs steadily, and you will need the proper waxing, strong arms, and willing lungs to make it to the top without stopping a few times to regroup the various aching parts of your body. The old road that you are climbing was at one time the main route between Boston and Albany. If the snow is not too deep you may notice a stone post on the right of the trail about ¼ mi. up from the parking area. The post marks the Massachusetts-New York state line. From now on, you are in New York State.

As the trail nears Berlin Pass there is one last steep stretch that will force you into a herringbone approach. Just when you have had enough and are beginning to wonder why you got interested in this madness in the first place, the trail levels out at the pass where it intersects with another trail running roughly north-south. This is Berlin Pass from which there is a fine view back towards Mt. Greylock in the east and over into New York in the west. But this view is just a taste of things to come.

Turn left (south) here and start skiing along another woods road that is part of the Taconic Crest Trail, which runs along the Taconic Range from just north of Pittsfield to its northern terminus well into Vermont. There are a few short level stretches in the first several hundred yards of this section of the trail, but soon the climbing begins again. Stick with it and think of the fine time you are going to have running back down this trail. The summit of Berlin Mtn. is 1¼ mi. from Berlin Pass.

As far as commanding panoramas go, the view from the top of Berlin Mtn. is as fine as any in Berkshire County. In my estimation it rates right up there with the views from the tops of Mt. Greylock, Mt. Everett, and Alander down in the southwestern corner of the county, and Tower Mtn. in Pittsfield State Forest. If the temperature is well below freezing and the wind is whistling out of the northwest, however, you will not want to spend too much time taking in the sights. There is very little shelter at the top and the wind slashes through to the bone, it seems. By the time you get to the top you will probably be perspiring freely from all the climbing. Do not give the wind a chance to turn this sweat into a layer of ice.

As you start down this and any other descent, keep in mind that you are not necessarily alone on the mountain. Remember to check your speed so that you are always in control, especially where you cannot see what or who is on the trail around the next corner. Also remember that a planned fall is a safe and sure way of stopping.

Chances are there will not be much traffic on this trail, and the run back to Berlin Pass and back down the old Boston-Albany Post Rd. will be a smooth one. It will surely be faster than the trip up, and I bet you find yourself considering making the climb—at least as far as the pass—just one more time.

BIBLIOGRAPHY

Appalachian Trail Conference. *Appalachian Trail Guide: Massachusetts-Connecticut*. Harpers Ferry, W. Va.; The Appalachian Trail Conference, 1977.

Birdsall, Richard D. *Berkshire County: A Cultural History*. New Haven: Yale Univ. Press, 1959.

Caldwell, John. *Cross-Country Skiing Today*. Brattleboro, Vt.: Stephen Greene Press, 1977.

Carney, William. *A Berkshire Sourcebook*. Pittsfield, Mass.: The Junior League of Berkshire County, 1976.

Federal Writers Project. *Berkshire Hills*. New York and London: Funk and Wagnalls, 1939.

Jorgensen, Neil. *A Guide to New England's Landscape*. Chester, Ct.: Pequot Press, 1977.

Peattie, Roderick, ed. *The Berkshires: The Purple Hills*. New York: Vanguard Press, 1948.

Smith, Chard Powers. *The Housatonic, Puritan River*. New York: Rinehart, 1946.

Thomson, Betty Flanders. *The Changing Face of New England*. Boston: Houghton Mifflin, 1977.

Williams Outing Club. *Williams Outing Club Trail Guide*. Williamstown, Mass.: Williams Outing Club, 1973.